Social Contacts

First published 1990 by
Prentice Hall International (UK) Limited
Campus 400, Maylands Avenue
Hemel Hempstead
Hertfordshire HP2 7EZ
A division of
Simon & Schuster International Group

Typeset in 10 pt Palacio
by MHL Typesetting Ltd, Coventry

Printed and bound in Great Britain
by Redwood Books, Trowbridge, Wiltshire

Library of Congress Cataloging-in-Publication Data

Brieger, Nick.
    Social contacts: materials for developing listening and speaking
skills in business and social contexts/Nick Brieger and Jeremy
Comfort.
    p.   cm.
    ISBN 0-13-816091-0: $8.50
    1. English language — Textbooks for foreign speakers. 2, English
language — Business English. 3. English language — Spoken English.
4. English language — Social aspects. 5. Listening. I. Comfort,
Jeremy. II. Title.
PE1128.B6738 1990
428.3'4 — dc20   89-49395
                                                                    CIP

British Library Cataloguing in Publication Data

Brieger, Nick, 1948–
    Social contacts: materials for developing listening and
    speaking skills in business and social contexts.
    Spoken English language
    I. Title   II. Comfort, Jeremy
    428.3

ISBN 0-13-816091-0

3 4 5 6 7   98 97 96 95 94

Contents

Introduction

Targets and objectives

This book is aimed at adults, at pre-intermediate levels and above, who need to develop and practise the language of social interaction for their studies, jobs or travels.

Listening passages act as input for tasks, focusing on both informational content and language content. In turn, this input is used as the basis for output tasks, focusing on speaking skills.

The listening materials are based around the following:

1. Face-to-face dialogues.
2. Short messages.
3. Telephone calls.

They develop the following skills:

1. Extracting relevant information.
2. Structuring information.
3. Inferring meaning from context.
4. Becoming accustomed to different varieties (formal and informal) and different accents of English.

The follow-up speaking activities develop communication skills through the following:

1. Problem-solving activities.
2. Role-plays.
3. Discussion topics.

Organisation of material

There are twenty units (see Contents). Each unit consists of:

Introduction

A short written introduction to the topic of the unit.

1. Listening

Taped material divided into two sections.

1.1 Information transfer

This consists of a number of short passages and is accompanied by information-transfer tasks.

1.2 Dilemma

This consists of one listening passage based around a dilemma. The students need to decide the most appropriate reaction — in terms of language or action or both. The following questions develop the unit theme by focusing on aspects of cross-cultural behaviour.

2. Presentation

This section highlights and explains language items from the listening passage.

3. Controlled practice

This section contains exercises to practise the language items introduced in the Presentation. It also includes exercises to develop vocabulary and introduces additional words and expressions related to the unit theme.

4. Transfer

This section contains communicative pair-work or group-work activities designed to encourage the students to use the language introduced and to practise it in a freer context.

The Key Section for each unit is in the second part of the book. It contains:

Listening (1)

A tapescript and answers to the information-transfer listening task.

Controlled practice (3)

Answers to the controlled-practice exercises.

Transfer (where necessary) (4)

Information for pair-work activities.

The roles of the teacher and the students

The materials provide the teacher with an opportunity to strike a balance between two classroom roles: teacher-controlled and teacher-monitored.

They also give students an opportunity for autonomous learning (self-study).

Sections 1, 2 and 3 (Listening, Presentation and Controlled practice) can be done with or without a teacher. Section 4 (Transfer) can be done by students in pairs or groups without a teacher, but some form of teacher monitoring is advisable.

Acknowledgements

The authors would like to thank their colleagues at Prentice Hall for their help in putting the finishing touches to this book.

Notes to the student

Who is *Social Contacts* for?

This material is for adults, who have some previous knowledge of English and need to develop language skills for business and social purposes. It can be used by students working alone; as self-study or homework during a general course; or as follow-up after a general course.

Selection of material

You can work through the material starting at Unit 1. Alternatively, you can choose units on the basis of the topic or language area (see Contents).

Using a unit

All of the units can be done without a teacher. All the sections in a unit can also be done without a teacher, but Listening 1.2 and the Transfer section are better done with a teacher.

Introduction

This tells you something about the subject of the unit.

1. Listening

The listening passages consist of two sections:

1.1 Information transfer

Short listening extracts accompanied by an information-transfer exercise.

1.2 Dilemma

Another short listening extract. Firstly, you are asked how you would react in the situation; then you are asked to discuss cultural differences based on the theme of the unit.

Instructions

    i Read through the introduction to the listening.
    ii Listen to all of the extracts in part 1.1 without stopping.
    iii As you listen, try to do the exercises.
    iv If necessary, listen to the tape again, stopping the tape and replaying sections.
    v Check your answers with the Key at the back of the book.
    vi If your answers to the first section are wrong, listen again. You can check the tapescript in the Key.
    vii Then listen to part 1.2. If you are working by yourself, you will need to think about how you would react in the situation.

2. Presentation

    i Read carefully through the presentation and explanation of the language area.
    ii Try to remember how this language was used on the tape. If you wish, listen to the tape again.

3. Controlled practice

    i Complete the exercises.
    ii Check your answers with the Key.
    iii If your answers are wrong, look again at the Presentation, and try to see why you have made mistakes.

4. Transfer

These activities involve speaking. You can do the pair-work speaking activities without a teacher. However, the transfer activities are best done with a teacher who can help you with your language.

    If you do the pair-work speaking activities with a colleague, follow this procedure:

    i Decide who is Student A and who is Student B.
    ii Student A should *only* look at the Student A copy.
    iii Student B should *only* look at the Student B copy in the Key Section.
    iv Carry out the Transfer activity. Try to use the language you have learnt.

Note: We have used the following symbols. They show you what is missing in the exercises:

In Section 1 (Listening) _ _ _ _ _ one or more words.
In Section 3 (Controlled practice) _ _ _ _ _ _ one or more words;
_____ only one word.

Teacher's notes

Uses of the material

1. As a complete course for adults who need English for social purposes.
2. As supplementary material to a General English course for students with an interest in or a need for English for social purposes.
3. As a self-study/homework component for a Social English course.
4. As follow-up material on completion of a General English course.

Selection of material

The units are not graded. Therefore teachers may select according to the following:

1. Topic (see Contents page).
2. Language Area (see Contents page).

Using a unit

Introduction

You can use the text as a basis for presenting the unit orally or for asking students to read it through themselves.

1. Listening

The input text for each unit is based on listening. The listening consists of two sections:

1.1 Information transfer

Short listening extracts accompanied by an information-transfer exercise.

1.2 Dilemma

Another short listening extract to which the student must react. The reaction is in terms of what is appropriate culturally. Some further questions are raised in order to encourage discussion of cross-cultural issues based on the unit theme.

Instructions:

    i Prepare the students for section 1.1 and the tasks. Make sure they are absolutely sure what they have to do.

    ii Play all the listening passages for the section, without stopping.

    iii For many students it will be necessary to give them an opportunity to listen to the tape text again. Stop the tape at appropriate places.

    iv Let the students check their answers using the Key.

    v Now play the tape for section 1.2. Ask the students how they would react in the situation presented. Discuss the cultural issues raised by the extract.

2. Presentation

    i Ask the students to read through the presentation and explanation of the language area.

    ii Get them to give you additional examples of the language presented.

    iii If necessary, look at the tapescript in the Key to identify exponents of the language.

3. Controlled practice

    i Ask the students to complete the exercises and then check their answers with the Key.

    ii Advise on alternative answers or give more practice where necessary.

4. Transfer

These activities involve speaking. Most of the speaking activities involve pair work.

    i Divide the class into pairs.

    ii Assign roles (Student A and Student B). Make sure they only look at their role/information (Student B's information is always in the Key Section).

    iii Monitor the pairs while they carry out the speaking transfer, prompting the use of practised language if necessary.

Note

The following symbols have been used to indicate what is missing in the exercises:

In Section 1 (Listening) _ _ _ _ _ one or more words.

In Section 3 (Controlled practice) _ _ _ _ _ one or more words;

_____ only one word.

First meetings 1

(greeting, introducing and acknowledging)

Introduction

In this unit a tour guide introduces herself to a group of tourists and also checks their details on her list.

1. Listening 🔲

1.1 Information transfer

You are going to hear four short dialogues. As you listen tick (✓) the names on the list and make any necessary corrections or changes.

⛰ Tyrol Tours

Resort: *Vienna* ✓   Representative: *Trish Graham*

Name		Length of stay	Hotel	Type of room
1. Ellis, George	☐	_ _ _ _ _ _ nights	_ _ _ _ _ _	Double
2. Ellis, Helen	☐	_ _ _ _ _ _ nights	_ _ _ _ _ _	Double
3. Lampola, _ _ _ _ _ _	☐	4 nights	The Casino	_ _ _ _ _ _
4. Newton, James	☐	10 nights	The Casino	Twin
5. Newton, _ _ _ _ _ _	☐	10 nights	The Casino	Twin
6. Itoh, Keiichi	☐	7 nights	_ _ _ _ _ _	Single

1.2 Dilemma

Now listen to the fifth dialogue.

1. How would you react if you were this tourist?
2. Each language has fixed expressions to greet people. How important is it to use the correct expression in your culture? What factors determine the greeting used (e.g. age, relationship, situation)?

---

2. Presentation

In the dialogues that you heard the speakers did the following:

greeted each other
introduced themselves or someone else
acknowledged information

Let's look at these in more detail.

2.1 Greetings and introductions

Often the greetings and the introductions follow this sequence:

greeting
introducing oneself or someone else
reply to introduction

Look at the following language.

1. Greeting and introducing oneself at the first meeting

Greeting	*Introducing oneself*	*Reply*
How do you do?	I'm ...	How do you do? I'm ...
Pleased to meet you.	My name is ...	Pleased to meet you, too. Mine's ...
Nice to meet you.		Nice to meet you, too.
Glad to meet you.		Glad to meet you, too.

Note
'How do you do?' is not really a question. It is not a request for information.

2. Greeting someone at the second and subsequent meetings

Greeting	Reply
How are you?	Very well, thanks. And you?
	Fine, thanks. And you?
	Not too bad./So-so./Could be worse.
	Not too good, I'm afraid.
	Absolutely awful/terrible/dreadful.

These greetings often come after the following exchange:

Greeting	Reply
Nice to see you.	Nice to see you, too.

Notes
1. The greeting 'How are you?' is a real question and request for information.
2. There is usually a difference between 'meet' for a first meeting and 'see' for a second and subsequent meeting, e.g. 'Pleased to meet you' (first time), 'Nice to see you' (subsequent time).
3. After 'Not too good, I'm afraid' and 'Absolutely awful/terrible/dreadful', it is common and polite for the other person to ask 'What's the matter/problem?'

3. Introducing oneself and getting on first-name terms

Introduction

My name is ...	Please call me ...
	You can call me ...

4. Introducing someone else

May I introduce ...?
I'd like to introduce ...
This is ...

2.2 Acknowledging information

When we exchange information in a conversation, we use short formulae or noises to indicate that we understand:

Formulae	Noises
OK	Uh-huh
Right	Mm
Fine	
I see	

3. Controlled practice

3.1

Look at the following exchanges and decide if they are appropriate or not; if they are inappropriate, correct them.

1. A: How do you do? My name's Peter Wallis.

    B: Pleased to meet you. Mine's Shirley Adams.

2. A: How do you do?

    B: I am very well thank you.

3. A: I am Frank Richards. Please call me Frank.

    B: Nice to see you. My name's Annabel Pilkington-Smythe. You can call me Ann. It's much simpler.

4. A: John, nice to see you. How are you?

    B: Not too good, I'm afraid. And you?

    A: I'm fine thanks.

5. A: May I introduce my husband John?

    B: Nice to meet you. My name's Sue Porter.

3.2

Now look at the following dialogue. The sentences are in the wrong order. Rearrange them into the correct order. The first sentence has been done for you.

JEAN: How do you do, Mr Coombs? ( )

JEAN: Please to meet you. Mine's Jean Braun. ( )

LIZ: Well, I think we all know each other now. So what about an aperitif? ( )

PAUL: Oh, please call me Paul. ( )

LIZ: How do you do? My name is Liz White. (*1*)

JEAN: OK. Fine. In that case please call me Jean. ( )

LIZ: And this is Paul Coombs, a colleague from work. ( )

4

4. Transfer

PAIR WORK

You are at a party. One of you is the host/ess; the other is a guest. You have not met before. Introduce yourselves.

GROUP WORK

You are at a party. One of you is the host/ess; the others are guests. The host/ess knows some of the guests. As host/ess you should:

    welcome and greet your guests
    introduce yourself to those you don't know
    introduce them to other guests at your party

First meetings 2

(presenting yourself)

Introduction

Encounter groups are therapy activities for people who want to solve their problems and improve their relationships with other people.

1. Listening |OO|──────────────────────

1.1 Information transfer

You are going to hear four short extracts from the first meeting of an encounter group. In this session the new participants present some information about themselves to the rest of the group. As you listen, link the names on the left with the information in the other columns. The first one has been done for you.

Name	Family	Job	Interests
Mary Wilkins	bachelor	research assistant	tennis
Paul Roberts	divorced + 2 children	actor	
George Evans	single	solicitor	theatre
Susanne Richards	grown-up children	secretary	

1.2 Dilemma

Now listen to the fifth extract.

1. How would you react?
2. It is said that some nationalities are typically more extrovert than others. As a result, people from those countries are better at interpersonal skills. Do you think that people in your culture find it easy to make initial contact with each other?
3. What do you think might be the reasons, in each case, for the person joining the group? Listen to the dialogues again, if necessary.

──────────────────────────────── |QO|

2. Presentation

In the dialogues, the encounter-group members presented themselves by giving their names, and relevant information about:

their family situation
their jobs
their interests

Let's look at some of the language they used.

2.1 Presenting your family situation

I'm single/married/divorced.
I'm a bachelor.
I've got one child.
I've got two grown-up children.

Note
'Bachelor' means an unmarried man; 'spinster' usually mean an (older) unmarried woman, but the term is used less and less nowadays.

2.2 Presenting your job

I work as a secretary. (job title)
I work in an insurance company. (job location)
I work for General Pharma. (name of employer)
I work for a chemical company. (sector of employer)
I'm on the technical side. (general area)
I'm in research and development. (specific activity or department)
I'm self-employed.
I'm retired.

2.3 Presenting your interests

I like the theatre and classical music.
I like travelling.
I play tennis and golf.

3. Controlled practice

3.1

Now look at the encounter-group notes about Allan, Geraldine and Lesley. Then complete the sentences about them.

Name	Family	Profession
Allan	bachelor	teacher/primary school
Geraldine	divorced/2 children	Marketing Manager/fashion magazine
Lesley	married/3 children	computers

1. Hello. My name is Allan. I'm _____. I _____ _____ a teacher _____ a primary school.
2. Good evening. I'm Geraldine. Please call me Gerry. I'm _____. I've _____ two children. I _____ the Marketing Manager _____ a fashion magazine.
3. Hello. My name is Lesley. I _____ _____. I've _____ three children. I _____ _____ computers.

3.2

A child greets his mother with the following expression:

'Hello, mum'.

'Mum' is a *form of address* between a child and its mother. Below are some other forms of address. Between which of the following people are they most appropriate? Link the people to the form of address. The first one has been done for you.

People	*Form of address*
1. you to a close male friend	a. Of course, dear.
2. you to a female acquaintance	b. Good evening.
3. you to stranger on the street	c. Your Majesty, ...
4. shop assistant to female customer	d. Hi, Tom.
5. you to hotel receptionist (upon arrival)	e. Hello, Mrs Mackintosh
6. you to close female colleague	f. Dear Mrs Fincham
7. between husband and wife	g. Hello, Mr Brown
8. you to the Queen	h. Excuse me
9. you to male acquaintance	i. See you, Mary!
10. you to a woman (in a letter)	j. Good morning, madam

4. Transfer

You are now going to present yourself at an encounter-group meeting. Each group should have a maximum of six members. Each person should:

give their name
present their family situation
describe their job
present their interests

UNIT 3 **Things in common**

(establishing contact)

Introduction

When two people (A and B) talk together for the first time, their conversation can look

like this: or like this:

A   B   A B
  Type 1   *Type 2*

In type 1 the speakers don't manage to establish contact because they don't get closer to each other; in type 2 each of the speakers moves in the direction of the other and towards closer contact.

1. Listening 🔘 ───────────────────────────────

1.1 Information transfer

You are going to hear four short dialogues. As you listen, decide whether the dialogue is like type 1 or type 2 above.

Dialogue 1   Type __

Dialogue 2   Type __

Dialogue 3   Type __

Dialogue 4   Type __

1.2 Dilemma

Now listen to the fifth dialogue.

1. How would you react?
2. In your country, is it acceptable to talk about how much money you earn and how much money you have?

───────────────────────────────────── 🔘

2. Presentation

A conversation is successful in establishing contact if the participants can find something in common in the topics they discuss. *Safe* topics vary from culture to culture. Here are some safe topics in the English-speaking world:

travel
jobs
interests
origins
weather

Let's look at some questions to start, and develop conversations about these topics.

2.1 Travel questions

Have you ever been to ... ?
Have you ever visited ... ?
Is this your first visit to ... ?
Where are you travelling/off to?

2.2 Job questions

So what do you do?
What do you do for a living?
What's your line of business?
So what exactly does your job involve?

2.3 Interests questions

Do you have any hobbies?
So what do you do in your spare time?
What do you enjoy/like doing in your spare time?
Do you like ... +ing?

2.4 Origin questions

Where do you come from? (country)
Where are you from? (country or town)
Where were you born? (country or town)
Where do you live? (country or town)

2.5 Weather questions

Nice/lovely day, isn't it?
Terrible weather, isn't it?
Whew, it's hot today, isn't it?
Brr, it's freezing outside, isn't it?

And now some responses to keep the conversation going.

2.6 Responses to interesting information

That's interesting.
How interesting!
Oh, really!

2.7 Responses to neutral information

Mm. I see.
Uh-huh.
Yes/Yeah.

2.8 Responses to sad information

What a shame/pity!
Oh dear.
Sorry to hear that.

3. Controlled practice

3.1

Here are some answers. What are the questions? The first one has been done for you.

1. _Where are you off to ?_ _ _ _ _ _ _ _ _ _ _ _ _ _ _ _ _ _ _

   We're off to Amsterdam.

2. _ tennis?

   Yes, very much. In fact I play at least once a week.

3. _ ?

   Well, I was born in England, but now I live in California.

4. _ Japan?

   Not yet. But I hope to get there one day.

5. So _ ?

   Well, actually I'm retired now.

6. _ _ _ _ _ _, _ _ _ _ _ _ _ _ _ _ _ _ _ _ _ _, isn't it?

   Absolutely boiling!

7. _
   _ _ _ _ _ _ _ _ _ _ _ _ _ _ _ _ ?

   In fact I don't have much spare time.

8. So _?

   Line of business? Well, I'm a brain surgeon.

3.2

Choose the most appropriate response from the choice given.

1. I come from a very small village in Finland — up near the Arctic circle.

    a. How interesting!
    b. I see.
    c. Oh dear.

2. The first train leaves at 6.30 in the morning.

    a. That's interesting.
    b. Uh-huh.
    c. I'm sorry to hear that.

3. Unfortunately my doctor says I mustn't drink any more alcohol.

    a. Oh, really!
    b. Yeah.
    c. What a pity!

4. Well, actually I was born in Buenos Aires.

    a. How interesting! I lived there for ten years myself.
    b. Uh-huh. I lived there for ten years myself.
    c. Oh dear. I lived there for ten years myself.

5. I used to play a lot of golf.

    a. Oh, really! Afraid I've never been too keen on it myself.
    b. Mm. I see. Afraid I've never been too keen on it myself.
    c. I am sorry to hear that. Afraid I've never been too keen on it myself.

3.3

Some other topics of conversation are less safe in English-speaking countries. If you want to introduce them, it is best to be indirect. Notice the indirect or careful way in which the following questions are asked and match them with the topic areas. The topic areas are:

age (A)
health (H)
money (M)
politics (P)
religion (R)

Would you mind if I asked how much you earn? ( )
I don't want to be inquisitive, but do you belong to a party? ( )
Forgive me for asking, but could you tell me your age? ( )
Are you by any chance a member of the church? ( )
How are things at the moment? ( )

How old are you, if you don't mind my asking? ( )
That's a beautiful dress. It must have cost the earth. ( )
I've often wondered about the troubles in your country. How is the situation at present? ( )
Excuse me for asking, but that medallion is the patron saint of travellers, isn't it? ( )
I heard that you weren't too well. I hope things are better now. ( )

3.4

Using the 'indirect formula' words below, rephrase the direct questions so that they are more polite or careful:

I hope you don't mind my asking, but . . .
Would you mind telling me . . .
It sounds awfully rude to ask, but . . .
Don't be offended, but . . .

1. How old is your husband?
2. Is your job well paid?
3. What do you think of your president?
4. You look terrible. Are you ill?
5. Are you married to that man?

4. Transfer

PAIR WORK

You are now going to practise establishing and maintaining contact around the following topics:

1. travel
2. jobs
3. interests
4. origins

Student A should start the conversation on topics 1 and 3; Student B should respond. Student B should start the conversation on topics 2 and 4; Student A should respond.

UNIT 4 **Origins 1**

(describing where you come from; comparisons)

Introduction

When we first meet someone we very often talk about our origins — where we come from. In this unit we will practise making comparisons about this subject, e.g.:

I live in Osaka. It's a big city but a lot smaller than Tokyo.

1. **Listening** 🔲

1.1 Information transfer

You are going to hear three short dialogues. As you listen complete the table.

Dialogue	Place of origin	Region	Compared with
1	Lille _ _ _ _ _ _	_ _ _ _ _ _ _ _ _ _ _ _	_ _ _ _ _ _ Other towns in South of Spain
2	_ _ _ _ _ _	North of England	_ _ _ _ _ _
3	Padua	_ _ _ _ _ _	_ _ _ _ _ _

1.2 Dilemma

Now listen to the fourth dialogue.

1. How would you react?
2. In some cultures a person's place of birth gives a strong feeling of *identity*; it gives the person a sense of having *roots*. Do people in your culture think that their roots are where they were born?

🔲

2. Presentation

In the dialogues you heard comparative and superlative adjectives formed in the following ways:

1. With *-er* and *the -est*
2. With *more* and *the most*

Let's look at these in more detail.

2.1 With *-er* and *the -est*

Lille is *smaller* than Paris. Lille is one of *the biggest* cities in the North of France. Milan is *bigger* than Padua. Padua is one of *the oldest* cities in Italy.

We also add *-er/-est* with adjectives ending in 'y': e.g. happ*ier*, ugl*iest*.

2.2 With *more* and *the most*

Padua is *more beautiful* than Milan. It's one of the *most beautiful* cities in Italy. York is *more attractive* than Oxford. It's one of the *most attractive* cities in England.

Notice also how we *strengthen* or *weaken* comparisons:

York is $\begin{Bmatrix} much \\ slightly \end{Bmatrix}$ more attractive than Oxford.

3. Controlled practice

3.1 Complete the table below:

Noun	Adjective	Opposite adjective
Size	big	_____
Beauty	_____	_____
Age	_____	_____
Noise	_____	_____
Industry	_____	_____
Interest	_____	_____
Proximity (to sea, etc.)	_____	_____

3.2

Now complete the following sentences, using the adjective in brackets.

1. Marbella is on the South coast of Spain. It's one of _ _ _ _ _ towns on this coast. (*attractive*)
2. I come from Dortmund. It's an industrial city in the North of Germany. It's much _____ than this little village. (*noisy*)
3. I live in York. It's much _____ than New York. (*old*)
4. I'm from a village near Edinburgh. It's much _ _ _ _ _ than living in the city. (*boring*)
5. He's from Boston. It's much _____ to New York than Washington. (*near*)
6. We come from Cairo. It's the _____ city in Egypt. (*big*)

3.3 Expressing location

In the North/South/East/West of ... (a country, region)
In the country/countryside (not in a town)
By the sea/on the coast
To the North/South/East/West of ... (a specific location)

Now look at the following map of the United Kingdom. Use the map to complete the sentences on the opposite page.

1. I come from Stevenage; it's _ _ _ _ _ London.
2. I live in Bristol; it's _ _ _ _ _ sea, _ _ _ _ _ London.
3. I come from Aberdeen; it's _ _ _ _ _ coast, _ _ _ _ _ Edinburgh.
4. I don't live in a town; I live _ _ _ _ _.
5. I come from Hastings; it's _ _ _ _ _ sea, _ _ _ _ _ England.
6. My parents come from Belfast; it's _____ Northern Ireland.

4. Transfer

Ask a colleague/friend where he/she comes from. Compare your origins.

Origins 2

(describing your home, place of work;
prepositions of place)

Introduction

When we are getting to know someone, we often talk about where we live and
what sort of house we live in, or describe the building where we work. In these
conversations we need to locate and describe our homes accurately.

1. Listening 𝄇

1.1 Information transfer

You are going to hear three dialogues in which people talk about their homes.
Match the picture of the home with the appropriate dialogue and list the particular
features you hear described.

Dialogue: ☐

Features: _ _ _ _ _ _

Dialogue: ☐

Features: _ _ _ _ _ _

Dialogue: ☐

Features: _ _ _ _ _ _

1.2 Dilemma

Now listen to the fourth dialogue.

1. How would you react?
2. In the United Kingdom, people usually don't know the size of their properties. They measure them in terms of number of bedrooms. In Japan accommodation is usually measured by mat size. Discuss the differences between the following typical property advertisement and one in your country.

Morgan & Melville

MM

Chartered Surveyors and Estate Agents

13 Station Road
Cambridge
Tel. 0223-333999

A BEAUTIFULLY MODERNISED THREE BEDROOMED SEMI-DETACHED PERIOD COTTAGE IN A QUIET VILLAGE, OVERLOOKING OPEN COUNTRYSIDE...

The property is very well situated in a pleasant road, among a fine mixture of period and modern houses. There are local shops, schools and a main-line station to London nearby. The village is not far from the beautiful market town of Saffron Walden.

The main features of the house include Full gas-fired central heating
● Two reception rooms ● Pine fitted kitchen ● Three bedrooms
● Parking space and attractive gardens to front and rear

---

2. Presentation

Notice how we use prepositions to locate places accurately by focusing on:

    static location
    dynamic location

2.1 Static location

at	at the front/at the back/at the side
	at the end/at the beginning
	at the top/at the bottom
on	on the river/on the border
	on the outskirts of town/on an estate
	on the seafront
	on the wall/on the first floor
in	in the mountains/in a wood
	in the country/town
	in the middle/centre
	in the suburbs
	in the room/in the building
near/by	near/by a river
	near/by the sea
	near/by the station

also:

inside/outside	outside town
above/below	above his flat
over/under	below the table
overlooking	overlooking the sea
surrounded	surrounded by hills
overlooked	overlooked by high-rise buildings
Note	
with	with a garden
	with a swimming pool

2.2 Dynamic location

to	Drive me to the station.
	I'm going to the theatre.
onto	We're building onto the back of the house.
into	The bus takes you into the city centre.
through	We are knocking through the wall.
across	We can see across the lake.
up/down	We're extending the house up into the attic.
	Walk down the hill to get to the station.

3. Controlled practice

3.1

Complete the following sentences with an appropriate preposition:

1. My office is _____ the third floor _____ the back of the building.

2. It's a bit noisy because it's right _____ the railway line.

3. We live just _____ town. It takes us ten minutes to get _____ the centre.

4. The man who lives _____ me plays the drums. I can hear the sound coming _____ the ceiling.

5. We're flying _____ Greece and we'll be staying _____ one of the islands.

6. There is a shed _____ the top of the garden.

7. He lives _____ the coast and can see _____ the channel on a fine day.

8. The building is _____ the corner _____ the end of the street.

3.2

Using the appropriate prepositions, invent some property descriptions from the lists provided.

Examples: A small house by a river, overlooking the park.
A dining room on the first floor, with an old fireplace.

detached house	suburbs	station
semi-detached house	outskirts	city centre
terraced house	housing estate	airport
flat/apartment	village	
bungalow	town	
cottage	country/countryside	
farmhouse	seafront	
	mountains	
	wood/forest	
	river	
	lake	

garden	dining room	central heating
patio	living room	fireplace
courtyard	bedrooms	french window
garage	study	
shed	kitchen	
swimming pool	bathroom	
conservatory	playroom	
greenhouse	hall	
orchard	landing	
vineyard	porch	
field	attic	

4. Transfer

Describe your home or office to a friend.

The day

(describing routines; present simple/frequency)

Introduction

We often need to inform others about our habits, e.g.:

I never drink coffee in the evenings.

We also often comment on differences in routines/habits, e.g.:

In Japan we always eat our main meal in the evening.
Really! Here we usually make lunch our main meal.

1. Listening oo

1.1 Information transfer

You are going to hear three dialogues. In each a time is fixed for a meal, an appointment or a meeting. As you listen, note the times:

Dialogue 1: Time of meeting: __ __ __ __ __

Dialogue 2: Time of lunch: __ __ __ __ __

Dialogue 3: Beginning time of meeting: __ __ __ __ __

End time of meeting: __ __ __ __ __

1.2 Dilemma

Now listen to the fourth dialogue.

1. How would you react?
2. Routines — both at work and at home — help to give us a sense of security. They enable us to achieve the maximum results from limited time and to organise our lives in an efficient way. Do you agree about the importance of routine?

2. Presentation

When we talk about habits, routines and characteristics, we use the *present simple* tense, as follows:

2.1 Statements

I *get up* at 6.30.
She *comes* to work by bike.
They *live* in a castle.

2.2 Questions

Where *do* you have lunch?
When *does* she get in to work?
Do they come from around here?

2.3 Negatives

The train *doesn't* leave till 8.
In Britain, we *don't* eat bread with the meal.

2.4 We also use *adverbs of frequency* in these types of sentences:

I *normally* start at 8.
I *never* get in before 9.
We *rarely* finish before 12.

3. Controlled practice

3.1

Order the following adverbs by placing them on the scale below:

most frequent   _____
                 _____
                 _____
                 _____
                 _____
                 _____
least frequent   _____

never, sometimes, often, usually, always, rarely, occasionally, seldom

3.2

Complete the dialogues:

Dialogue 1
A: When _ _ _ _ _ usually _ _ _ _ _ ?
B: Oh about 7.
A: Do you want a call in the morning?
B: No, I always _ _ _ _ _ before 7.

Dialogue 2
A: Are you hungry?
B: No, I rarely _____ lunch.
A: Really! You mean nothing at all?
B: Yes. I never _____ the time.

Dialogue 3
A: _____ he _____ round here?
B: No, he _____. He _____ in Spain.
A: So why _____ he _____ here every year?
B: I'm not sure. They say he _ _ _ _ _ for the beer!

3.3

To express a habit or routine we often use *to be used to doing something*.

Examples: We're used to getting up early,
I'm used to finishing work late.

To express the idea of getting a new habit we often use *to get used to doing something*.

Examples: I'm getting used to the late lunches.
You'll have to get used to leaving late.

However, to express the idea of something we no longer do, we use *used to do*.

Examples: I used to live in the city. (I don't anymore)
We used to work together. (We don't anymore)

Complete the following sentences:

1. I _ _ _ _ _ in London. I now live in Edinburgh.
2. It's hard to get up early but I _ _ _ _ _ it.
3. He'll help you write the letter. He _ _ _ _ _ letters.
4. I _ _ _ _ _ hate living in the country. I now rather enjoy it.
5. He doesn't like having to go to school but he _ _ _ _ _ it.

4. Transfer

1. Describe your day (at work and at home) to your partner.
2. Ask and answer questions with your partner about other business-related situations. Use these ideas to start with:

> manage to do some sight-seeing
> use telex or fax
> try local food when travelling overseas
> use a lap-top computer when travelling by air or rail
> attend trade fairs

UNIT 7 **The date**

(making and confirming arrangements)

Introduction

In this unit we are going to practise fixing an appointment over the telephone.

1. Listening ▭

1.1 Information transfer

You are going to hear three telephone calls between Peter and Ron. They are trying to arrange a round of golf. As you listen, complete the notes:

Call 1:   Day and time fixed: _ _ _ _ _

Call 2:   Reason for cancelling: _ _ _ _ _ _

Call 3:   Day and time fixed: _ _ _ _ _ _

1.2 Dilemma

Now listen to the fourth extract.

1. How would you react?
2. Time and punctuality are more important in some cultures than in others. What are the attitudes in your country?

▭

2. Presentation

In the telephone calls the speakers discussed:

their future fixed plans
their future intentions
their future schedules
future certainties/expressing willingness

Now let's look at the language they used.

2.1 Future fixed plans

I'm *flying* to the States/I'm *going* to London.

Here we use the present continuous tense.

2.2 Future intentions

I'm *going to be* pretty busy.

Here we use *to be going to* + infinitive.

2.3 Future schedules

On Saturday the flight *leaves* at 14.00.
When *does* the film *start*?

Here we use the present simple.

2.4 Future certainties/expressing willingness

I'll see you there/I'll call you back
I *won't* be able to make it
I'll do it (instead of you).

Here we use the future with *will*.

3. Controlled practice

3.1

Read through this dialogue. Correct any of the verbs which you think sound wrong/unnatural:

A: What do you do next Saturday?

B: Oh, I don't know. I haven't decided. What about you?

A: I'll go to the cinema in the evening.

B: Oh, what are you seeing?

A: A film called 'A Fish called Wanda'.

B: Oh I'd like to see that. What time is it starting?

A: At 8, I think. I'm going to check and give you a ring.

B: Thanks. I'll speak to you later then. Bye.

A: Bye.

3.2

Create dialogues to match the following:

1. A suggests a game of tennis, Friday 4 p.m.
   B can't make it. Next Friday is free.

2. A invites B to a business breakfast at A's hotel.
   B agrees and suggests a time and place to meet.

3. A asks B to the ballet next Friday.
   B asks what time it starts and A replies.
   B has another engagement.

4. A talks about her schedules for the coming week.
   B arranges to see A for lunch on Wednesday.

3.3

Here are some headings and expressions for making appointments and fixing dates. Put expressions 1–6 below under a suitable heading.

A. Suggesting an appointment/date

What about a round of golf?
How about a drink this evening?

— — — — —

B. Suggesting a time

Could you manage Tuesday?
Are you free in the afternoon?

— — — — —

— — — — —

C. Rejecting the suggestion

I'm sorry, I can't make Tuesday.
Unfortunately I'm busy that day.

— — — — —

D. Accepting the suggestion

That's fine.

— — — — —

E. Confirming the arrangement

I'll see you there at 2 o'clock.

— — — — —

1. All right.
2. Would Saturday suit you?
3. I look forward to seeing you then.
4. Why don't we go to the cinema?
5. I'm afraid Tuesday's out of the question.
6. Shall we say 2 o'clock?

4. Transfer

1. **Student B**: Turn to the Key section.
    Student A: Phone student B. Try to arrange a meeting next week. Here is your diary:

Monday: 13	*10.30 Flight to Munich* *Meetings in Munich and Nurenburg*
Tuesday: 14	*12.00 Flight → LONDON* *14.00 Meeting with boss*
Wednesday: 15	*Drive to factory* *p.m. factory inspection*
Thursday: 16	*9.00 A.M. meeting with customer* *11.00 Train to exhibition in Manchester*
Friday: 17	*14.00 Golf with Ron*

2. **Student A**: Telephone student B. Ask to speak to Ron Kent. You want to cancel your golf game on Friday.

Interests

(expressing likes, indifference, dislikes)

___

Introduction

In general conversation and after a performance (play, film, concert, etc,) we often talk about our likes and dislikes.
We can express these generally: e.g. 'I enjoy skiing'
or as an immediate response: e.g. 'I thought it was fantastic'

1. Listening ⟨oo⟩

1.1 Information transfer

You are going to hear two dialogues: the first about general likes/dislikes, the second following the performance of a play. As you listen, fill in the boxes below:
Use these symbols: ✓✓ = like a lot
✓ = quite like
0 = indifference
X = dislike

Dialogue 1

Ron speaks first:

Subject	James	Joan	Ron	Sandra
Restaurants	☐	☐	☐	☐
Pubs	☐	☐	☐	☐

Dialogue 2

Peter speaks first, Susan last:

Subject	Maria	Peter	Günther	Susan
Play	☐	☐	☐	☐

1.2 Dilemma

Now listen to the third dialogue.

1. How would you react?
2. Saying 'no' in this situation is difficult. Is it easy to decline offers in your country? What would people say in this situation?

---

2. Presentation

In the dialogues the speakers expressed:

their likes
their indifference
their dislikes

The speakers made:

a general statement

or

an immediate response

Now look at the language they used.

2.1 General statements

General statements about likes and dislikes or responses to 'What do you think/feel about ...?'

Likes	Indifference	Dislikes
I (really) like to/ ... ing	I don't mind ... ing	I don't like ...
I enjoy ... ing	I'm not too fond of ... ing	I dislike ... ing
I love to/ ... ing	(It was) all right	I hate to/ ... ing
I'm keen on ... ing		I can't stand ... ing

2.2 Immediate responses

Responding to

'What did you think of it?'
'(I thought) it was ...'

Likes (✔✔)	Quite likes (✔)	Indifference (0)	Dislikes (X)
fantastic	quite nice	not bad	terrible
superb	rather good	okay	awful
marvellous		all right	horrible
tremendous			ghastly
excellent			disgusting
terrific			revolting (only food)
delicious (only food)			

3. Controlled practice

3.1

Use the symbols in brackets to respond to the questions:
1. A: Do you enjoy watching TV?
    B: _ _ _ _ _ sometimes (0)

2. A: What did you think of the film?
    B: _ _ _ _ _ (✔✔)

3. A: What do you think of sport on TV?
    B: Oh, _ _ _ _ _ (X)

4. A: What did you think of the meal?
    B: _ _ _ _ _ (✔✔)

5. A: What's your favourite hobby?
    B: _ _ _ _ _ sailing (✔)

6. A: What did you think of the wine?
   B: _ _ _ _ _ (0)

7. A: What do you think of English food?
   B: _ _ _ _ _ (X)

8. A: What did you think of the concert?
   B: _ _ _ _ _ (X)

9. A: Do you like the climate here?
   B: Yes, _ _ _ _ _ the summers (✓✓)

10. A: I enjoyed his last book, didn't you?
    B: Well, actually, _ _ _ _ _ (X)

3.2

Exchanges like these can start off a conversation but the next step usually involves an exchange of reasons. Look at exercise 3.1 again and choose a suitable reaction from speaker A to B's response. Use this list:

(a) Oh, I thought it was rather exciting.
(b) Why especially?
(c) What else do you do?
(d) It's a pity we were sitting so far back. I could hardly hear.
(e) I agree. I've tasted much better!
(f) Yes, I enjoyed it too.
(g) How do you think it could be improved?
(h) I agree with you. It's quite tasteless.
(i) Yes, but how do you find the winters?
(j) Really? That's interesting. I like watersports too.

4. Transfer

1. Below is a sample list of hobbies and interests. Some have been left out. Decide which category to put them under.

   Handicrafts: knitting, sewing, cabinet-making, furniture-restoring

   Do-it-yourself (DIY): decorating, rebuilding, extending

   Games: bridge, backgammon

   Outdoor: walking, swimming, gliding

   Racket sports: tennis, squash

   Ball sports: rugby, football (soccer), handball, basketball, volleyball

   Other sports: hockey, fishing, climbing, parachuting

   Evening entertainment: cinema, theatre, concerts, pubs, night-clubs, discotheques

hang-gliding, netball, opera, dress-making, rambling, chess, badminton, renovating, pottery, picture-framing

Can you add any others?

PAIR WORK

2. Discuss with a partner your likes and dislikes generally. If you like, you can use the list above.
3. Discuss with a partner a recent film/play/book that you both know.

UNIT 9 **Entertainment 1**

(offering, refusing and accepting)

Introduction

Before a meal, during an interval at the theatre or in a bar, it is usual to offer
to buy drinks. Your guests will respond appropriately.

1. Listening 🔲

1.1 Information transfer

You are going to hear an exchange in a theatre bar during the interval. As you
listen, complete the table below.

Drinks order:

Person	First round	Second round
Francesca	_____	_____
Jeremy	_____	_____
Jane	_____	_____
Robert	_____	_____

1.2 Dilemma

Now listen to the second dialogue.

1. How would you react?
2. In social situations you often need to refuse invitations. In your country do you need to give excuses? What types of excuses or reasons are acceptable in your culture?

---

2. Presentation

In the dialogues you heard people offering and responding.

Offering	→	*Responding*
How about a (drink)?	→	Good idea.
What about a (drink)?	→	That would be nice.
Would you like a (drink)?	→	Yes please.
	→	No thanks/thank you.
	→	I'd love to but → I'm busy, etc.
	→	I'm afraid I can't.
What would you like?	→	I'd like (a gin and tonic).
	→	I'll have (a beer)
	→	Mine's (a whisky).

Offering to pay: Let me get this one/these.
This/These is/are on me.
This is my round. (for drinks only)

3. Controlled practice

3.1

What would you say in the following situations:

1. You want to suggest a coffee break.

   —

2. You want to offer a biscuit/piece of cake.

   —

3. You're hungry and somebody says: 'How about lunch?'

   —

4. You're very busy and somebody says: 'Would you like to join me for lunch?'

   _____

5. You want to find out what your guests want to drink.

   _____

6. You want to find out what your guests want to eat.

   _____

7. You're thirsty and somebody says: 'Would you like a beer?'

   _____

8. Your host is offering to buy the meal. You want to repay him for all his help.

   _____

9. Your host has bought the first round of drinks. You would like to buy the next round.

   _____

10. You arrive as a guest at someone's house. You're tired and dirty. Your host says: 'Would you like a shower?'

   _____

3.2

Express the following without changing the meaning but using the words in brackets:

1. I'll pay. (*round*)

2. I think we should have a drink. (*how about*)

3. I'll have a lager. (*mine's*)

4. I want to pay. (*get*)

3.3

Here are some excuses you could use to *leave* a social event:

1. Business/appointments
    I'd love to stay but I've got another appointment.
                    I must rush.
                    I've got a lot on at the moment.

2. Illness
    I'm afraid I must leave; I've got a terrible headache.
                    I don't feel very well.
                    I feel a bit ...

Other excuses are possible in other situations.
  Use the following excuses to decline an invitation to go to a film this evening:

(a) You haven't seen your family for several days.

_____

(b) You are very tired.

_____

(c) You saw the film last week.

_____

(d) Your car is being repaired.

_____

4. Transfer

SMALL GROUP WORK

Take it in turns to be the host offering to buy drinks.

PAIR WORK

Student B: Turn to the Key Section.
Student A: Student B will make offers in a variety of situations. In each
             case, decline the offer and make excuses.

UNIT 10 Travel 1

(requesting information)

Introduction

In this unit you are going to hear some short conversations about travel and travel arrangements.

1. Listening 🔲

1.1 Information transfer

You are going to hear six short dialogues. Each dialogue refers to a different type of transport. As you listen, write down the type of transport and the destination required. The first one has been done for you.

Dialogue	Type of transport	Destination
1	_Bus_	_Superstore_
2		
3		
4		
5		
6		

1.2 Dilemma

Now listen to the seventh dialogue.

1. How would you react?
2. On the one hand we are assured that travel has never been safer; on the other hand newspapers regularly inform us about serious accidents. What is considered the safest and most efficient means of transport in your country?

---

2. Presentation

In each of the dialogues that you heard, the traveller requested information. The requests were:

    introductory requests
    direct questions
    indirect questions

Let's look at these in more detail.

2.1 Introductory requests

An introductory request states the topic that the speaker wants to ask about.

I'd like to enquire about flights to Paris.
I'd like to ask about the total on the invoice.

2.2 Direct questions

Direct questions ask for specific information. The direct questions in the dialogues all started with a WH-question word.

Question word	Information requested
Who?	people
What?	thing
Which?	thing
Where?	place
When?	time
Why?	reason
How?	manner
How long?	length of time
How much/many?	quantity and amount

2.3 Indirect questions

Indirect questions also ask for specific information — but in a more polite way. The indirect questions in the dialogues started with a polite expression.

Could you tell me how often they go?
I'd like to know why there is a supplement.

Note
There is no inversion after indirect questions: i.e. Can you tell me *where the station is?* NOT Can you tell me *where is the station?*

3. Controlled practice

3.1

In the following telephone conversation, A is an assistant in a travel bureau. First, number the sentences in the correct order; then add an appropriate WH-question word in the gaps provided. The conversation is divided into two sections.

Section 1

A: I see. One moment, sir. Yes, there are four flights out. ( )
A: Yes, sir, and _____ is it for? ( )
A: Good morning. Preston Travel. (**1**)
B: _____ do they leave from? ( )
B: Out on Wednesday 12 April and back on Thursday 13. ( )
B: Yes, good morning. I'd like to enquire about flights to Italy. ( )
A: They're from London Heathrow. ( )
A: Yes, sir. _____ exactly would you like to fly to? ( )
B: To Milan. ( )

Section 2

A: The return flight leaves Milan at 17.30 and arrives back in Manchester at 20.30. ( )
A: From Manchester there's just one flight a day — leaving at 8.30 in the morning. ( )
B: _____ long for? ( )
A: 14.30. ( )
B: Back at 20.30. That sounds better. ( )
A: And _____ time does it arrive in Milan? ( )
A: Er, yes, because there's a stopover in Heathrow. ( )
A: Er, one hour. ( )
B: _____ do you have from Manchester? (**10**)
B: OK. And back? ( )
B: 14.30! _____ does it take so long? ( )

3.2

Use the expressions in the box to make polite, indirect questions from the direct questions 1–10. The notes in the box will help you.

Can you tell me ...? I'd like to know ...	Use with questions that ask for information.
Can you tell me if ...? Do you know if ...?	Use with questions that require a yes/no answer.

44

1. What time does the plane leave?
2. Where is the hotel, exactly?
3. How much does it cost?
4. When do we visit Versailles?
5. Do I have to get a visa?
6. Is the insurance included in the cost?
7. How much is the cancellation fee?
8. Does the room have a private bathroom?
9. Is there a swimming pool?
10. What is the time difference?

4. Transfer

PAIR WORK

Student B: Turn to the Key Section.
Student A: You have just started a new job as a travel assistant in a travel agency. Student B phones you to ask about flights from London to Bangkok.

Here is the relevant section from the timetable. Ask when approximately he/she wants to travel. Ask which day of the week he/she wants to travel. Respond to Student B's questions.

London to Bangkok				
Days	Depart	Arrive	Flight number	Stops
1234567				
2 4 6	10.00	06.45 +	TG815	1 (Bombay)
5	10.00	07.00 +	TG917	1 (Dhaka)
1	11.00	07.45 +	TG913	1 (Delhi)
7	11.45	06.25 +	TG919	0
34 6	12.00	06.45 +	BA009	0
1 5	15.35	12.45 +	BA033	1 (Bahrain)

Notes
1 Monday, 2 Tuesday, 3 Wednesday, 4 Thursday, 5 Friday, 6 Saturday, 7 Sunday
+ Next day   BA British Airways   TG Thai Airways International

Travel 2

(expressing permission and obligation)

Introduction

In this unit you are going to hear some conversations about problems concerned with travel.

1. Listening ⌒⌒

1.1 Information transfer

You are going to hear two dialogues. In the first dialogue an air passenger has just arrived at London Heathrow airport but his luggage has not arrived. Imagine that you are the official, and complete the form below.

```
┌─────────────────────────────────────────────────────────────────────────┐
│                              Luggage claim                                │
│                                                                           │
│   Passenger's name: _ _ _ _ _ _ _ _ _ _ _ _ _ _ _ _ _ _ _ _ _ _          │
│   Arriving from: _ _ _ _ _ _ _ _ _ _ _ _ _ _ _ _ _ _ _ _ _ _ _ _         │
│   Flight number: _ _ _ _ _ _ _ _ _ _ _ _ _ _ _ _ _ _ _ _ _ _ _           │
│   Passenger's contact address: _ _ _ _ _ _ _ _ _ _ _ _ _ _ _ _ _         │
│                                  _ _ _ _ _ _ _ _ _ _ _ _ _ _ _ _ _        │
│                                  _ _ _ _ _ _ _ _ _ _ _ _ _ _ _ _ _        │
│   Contact telephone number: _ _ _ _ _ _ _ _ _ _ _ _ _ _ _ _ _ _          │
│   Delete as appropriate                                                   │
│   Claim for damage/loss                                                   │
│   Description of luggage:                                                  │
│   1. _ _ _ _ _ _ _ _ _ _ _ _ _ _ _ _ _ _ _ _ _ _ _ _ _ _                 │
│   2. _ _ _ _ _ _ _ _ _ _ _ _ _ _ _ _ _ _ _ _ _ _ _ _ _ _                 │
│   3. _ _ _ _ _ _ _ _ _ _ _ _ _ _ _ _ _ _ _ _ _ _ _ _ _                   │
│   Passenger's signature: _ _ John Francks _ _ _ _ _ _ _ _                 │
│   For official use only                                                   │
│   Signature: _ Paul Rowan _ Date: _23 August 1990_ _                      │
└─────────────────────────────────────────────────────────────────────────┘
```

Now listen to the second dialogue. You are the passenger. Make notes about your travel arrangements on the memo pad below.

```
Notes

Departure time: _ _ _ _ _ _ _ _ _ _

Arrival time: _ _ _ _ _ _ _ _ _ _ _

Flight: _ _ _ _ _ _ _ _ _ _ _ _ _

Departure from: _ _ _ _ _ _ _ _ _ _
```

1.2 Dilemma

Now listen to the third dialogue.

1. How would you react?
2. The word 'officialdom' describes 'the (often unhelpful) attitude or behaviour of officials'. How are officials regarded in your country? Do they occupy a special position or have special status?

2. Presentation

In the dialogues the speakers

    expressed obligation
    asked, gave and refused permission

Let's look at these in more detail.

2.1 Expressing obligation

The idea of obligation can be divided into the following three notions:

1. Obligation to do something

Citizens *must* have a valid visa.
I*'ve got to* be in Milan for a meeting at three.
You'll *have to* fill in this form.
I *need to* have your signature.

2. Obligation not to do something (prohibition)

I really *mustn't* miss that appointment.
Citizens *are not allowed to* enter the country without a visa.

3. No obligation to do something

You *needn't* worry, sir.
We *don't need to* have a visa to visit Britain.
I *didn't have to* have one two weeks ago.
I *haven't got to* let you in at all.

2.2 Asking, giving and refusing permission

1. Asking permission

May I ask for your full name, sir?
Can I just see your ticket?
Do you mind if I just think that over for a moment?

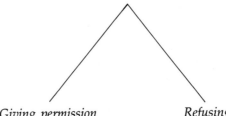

2.   *Giving permission*   *Refusing permission*

After 'may' or 'can'

Yes, of course you may/can.   No, you can't/may not.
Yes, certainly.   I'm afraid not.

After 'do you mind?'

No, not at all.   Well, I'd rather you didn't.
No, please do.

3. Controlled practice

3.1 Obligation

Rewrite the following sentences to make them sound less formal. Use the verb form in brackets in the appropriate tense. The first one has been done for you.

1. It is necessary for you to have a valid visa. (*must*)

   _ _ *You must have a valid visa* _ _ _ _ _ _ _ _

2. It won't be necessary to confirm your reservation. (*need to*)

   You _

3. I'm sorry, but it isn't possible to take that bag on the plane. (*allowed*)

   I'm sorry, but you _ _ _ _ _ _ _ _ _ _ _ _ _ _ _ _ _

4. It is essential for me to be on the 9 o'clock flight. (*must*)

   I _

5. The direct flight was cancelled; so it was necessary to come via Frankfurt. (*have to*)

   The direct flight was cancelled; so I _ _ _ _ _ _ _ _ _ _ _ _ _ _

6. I'm sorry, but cigar smoking is not allowed here. (*mustn't*)

   I'm sorry, but you _ _ _ _ _ _ _ _ _ _ _ _ _ _ _ _ _

7. Can I use your phone? It is essential for me to call the office. (*got to*)

   Can I use your phone? I _ _ _ _ _ _ _ _ _ _ _ _ _ _ _ _

8. That's OK. It's not necessary to pay. (*needn't*)

   That's OK. You _ _ _ _ _ _ _ _ _ _ _ _ _ _ _ _ _ _ _

3.2 Permission

Link each request (1–5) with the most appropriate response (a–e).

1. May I speak to Mr Smith, please?
2. Do you mind if I connect you to his secretary?
3. Can I see your ticket, please?
4. Do you mind if I join you?
5. May I buy you a drink?

a. Well, I'd rather you didn't; my husband will be here any minute.
b. Yes, certainly. Here you are.
c. I'm afraid not; he's away all this week.
d. Yes, of course you may. Thank you.
e. No, not at all. Please do.

49

4. Transfer

PAIR WORK

1. **Student B**: Turn to the Key Section.
   Student A: You have booked an APEX economy seat on a plane to New York for a two-week stay from 1 July. Because of an important engagement you now want to change the arrangements. You would prefer to cancel the flight and get your money back. If you can't get your money back then the earliest you can go is 15 July for two weeks.

   Ring the travel agent (Student B) and

   explain the situation
   make your request

2. **Student A**: You arrived in John F. Kennedy airport in New York one hour ago on flight TW167 from Paris. All the other passengers have collected their luggage and gone. Your luggage has not arrived. You go to the 'Baggage Claims' desk and ask about your luggage.

Health

(describing your symptoms; sequencing)

Introduction

Unfortunately, we sometimes become ill when we are away from home. It may be necessary to go to the doctor or to a pharmacist.

1. Listening 🔘

1.1 Information transfer

You are going to hear two conversations in a doctor's surgery. As you listen, complete the table below:

Patient	Illness	Duration	Other symptoms	Diagnosis	Advice/ prescription
1	_ _ _ _ _	_ _ _ _ _	_ _ _ _ _	_ _ _ _ _	_ _ _ _ _
2	_ _ _ _ _	_ _ _ _ _	_ _ _ _ _	_ _ _ _ _	_ _ _ _ _

1.2 Dilemma

Now listen to the third dialogue.

1. How would you react?
2. What is the attitude to 'alternative' medicine in your country? Do you believe in it?

🔘

2. Presentation

Opening question: What's the matter/problem?

Describing symptoms: I've got a (headache/stomach ache/pain in my .../sore ...)
I've been getting (pains in the ...)

Duration: When did it start?
How long have you been getting them/suffering from ...

Other symptoms: (Have you had) any other symptoms?

Examination: Let's have a look at ...

Diagnosis: It could be ... (possibility)
It's probably ... (probability)
It's ... (certainty)

Advice: You should ...
You had better ...

Prescription: I'm going to write/give you a prescription.
(I'd like you to) take these once/twice a day.
one after meals.
two in the morning/afternoon/before you go to bed.
every four hours.
three times a day.

3. Controlled practice

3.1

Match items in the following columns to practise expressing symptoms with these sentences:

I've got a ...
I feel ...
I've got a pain in my ...

sick	sore	neck
dizzy	stiff	eye
faint	broken	ankle
tired	sprained	arm
depressed	swollen	temperature
	bloodshot	headache
	high	stomach ache
	bad	finger
	runny	throat
		cold
		cough
		nose
		rash

3.2

Situation 1

You have suffered from a pain in your chest for the last two days. You have no other symptoms. You decide to visit the doctor's. Complete the dialogue:

DR: What's the matter?

YOU: _ _ _ _ _

DR: How long have you had it?

YOU: _ _ _ _ _

DR: Have you got any other symptoms?

YOU: _ _ _ _ _

DR: Right, let's have a look. . . . (carries out examination) There doesn't seem to be anything serious. It _____ be a chest infection. Just in case, _ _ _ _ _ a prescription. _ _ _ _ _ one tablet twice a day.

Situation 2

You have had a fever for the last three days. You have also been aching all over. You have lost your appetite. You decide to visit a doctor. Complete the dialogue:

DR: Right, what's the problem?

YOU: _ _ _ _ _

DR: When did it start?

YOU: _ _ _ _ _

DR: Have you had any other symptoms?

YOU: _ _ _ _ _

DR: Well, it sounds as though you've got a bug. You should get plenty of rest and drink lots of fluid.

YOU: _ _ _ _ _

DR: No, the best thing in these cases is to take nothing — let it run its course.

3.3

Label the drawing below. Choose from the following list of words:

chest, thigh, hip, ankle, wrist, shoulder, elbow, toes, throat, waist, calf

Complete any others you know.

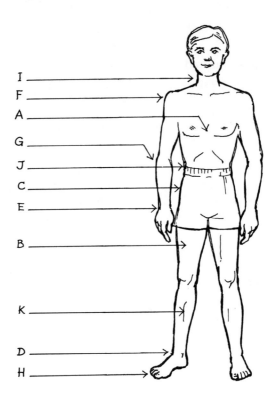

I _____
F _____
A _____
G _____
J _____
C _____
E _____
B _____
K _____
D _____
H _____

4. Transfer

PAIR WORK

Take on the role of either doctor or patient. Act out three visits to the doctor based on illnesses/injuries as listed above.

Shopping

(finding out about availability)

Introduction

Finding the right shop and then finding exactly what you want to buy can be difficult. Good contacts with people in the streets and in the shops will make it easier.

1. Listening 🔘

1.1 Information transfer

You are going to hear two visitors making contact while shopping. As you listen, complete the table:

Visitor	Type of shop	Item bought	Price	Method of payment
1	_ _ _ _ _ _	_ _ _ _ _ _	_ _ _ _ _	_ _ _ _ _
2		_ _ _ _ _	_ _ _ _ _	_ _ _ _ _

1.2 Dilemma

You are now going to hear two customers return to shops. They are going to try to get their money back.

1. How would you react in the second situation?
2. In your country do customers always have the right to get their money back in these situations?

---

2. Presentation

2.1 Finding the right shop

Can you tell me where I can find ... (a pharmacy, etc.)
Is their somewhere I can find ... (shetland pullovers, etc.)
Can you recommend somewhere to buy ... (a video-recorder, etc.)

2.2 Finding the right counter/part of shop

Excuse me, I'm looking for ... (gloves/the menswear department)

2.3 Asking for help from the shop assistant

I wonder if you could help me. I'd like to get ...
I'm not sure about ... (the colour, size, etc.)

2.4 Making comments

Oh no, that's too expensive/not big enough
That's very nice/pretty/just what I wanted.

2.5 Method of payment

Can I pay by cheque (*check*: American spelling)/traveller's cheques?
Do you accept Visa/Mastercard/etc.?

2.6 Receiving the goods

Here you are, madam/sir, and there's the receipt.
Don't forget your receipt, sir/madam.

2.7 Returning goods

I'd like my money back on this garment. It's too small.
It's shrunk.
It's broken.
I'd like to exchange this for a larger one.

3. Controlled practice

3.1

Match the shopper's questions/statements with the responses of the shop assistant/stranger in the street:

Shopper's questions/statements

1. That's too expensive.
2. Do you accept any credit cards?
3. Can you tell me where I can find a greengrocers?
4. Excuse me, I'm looking for the children's clothes.
5. That's just what I've been looking for.
6. Is there somewhere I can buy second-hand records?
7. I wonder if you could help me. I wonder if you have this in any other colours?
8. Can you recommend somewhere good for ladies' shoes?
9. I'd like my money back on this pullover. It's too big.
10. I'd like to see the manager.

Responses

(a) Um ... yes, I believe there's a music shop on Parliament Street.
(b) Of course, madam. If you'd like to come this way, I'll show you ...
(c) Have you got a receipt?
(d) Yes, we take Visa and Access.
(e) Just a moment, I'll get him.
(f) Perhaps you'd be interested in these. They're slightly cheaper
(g) Oh I am glad, madam.
(h) Umm ... yes. Try Bally's. They're just over the bridge, first left.
(i) Yes, go straight down the hill and you'll see a fruit shop on your left.
(j) You'll find them on the second floor sir.

3.2

Construct suitable sentences for the following situations, using the words in brackets:

1. You want a new battery for your calculator. (*Can you tell me where ...*)
2. You don't necessarily want to buy something in the shop you are in. (*... looking*)
3. A pair of shoes you are trying on are too small. (*enough*)
4. The item you're looking at is very dear. (*rather more reasonable*)
5. The goods you have bought are faulty. (*refund*)

3.3

Construct suitable sentences from the following tables. What clothes could they refer to?

It is They are	too	long big short large baggy small tight wide	in on round	the leg. the shoulders. the arms. the hips. the chest. the bottom.

Can I have	it them	shortened lengthened taken in let out altered	?

Have you got	it one them something	(in)	smaller larger shorter longer red another colour another size	?

3.4 Types of shops

Food shops: butcher's, baker's, grocer's, greengrocer's, delicatessen, supermarket
Clothes shops: men's shop, women's shop, department store, shoe shop
Others: ironmonger's (hardware store), pharmacist's (chemist's: British English),
bookshop, newsagent's

In which type of shop would you buy the following?

(a) a kilo of beef
(b) a packet of cigarettes
(c) a hammer
(d) half a kilo of tomatoes
(e) a suit
(f) a skirt
(g) some toothpaste
(h) some pickled olives

4. Transfer

PAIR WORK

Student B: Turn to the Key Section.
Student A: You would like to buy an alarm clock. you have been directed to
a large department store:

1. Find out which part of the shop to go to.
2. Explain what you want, find out prices and types, decide which
one to buy.

UNIT 14 **Food and drink 1**

(booking, ordering, complaining)

Introduction

This unit focuses on the social contacts in a restaurant — in particular how the host/hostess helps his/her guests choose from the menu.

1. Listening

1.1 Information transfer

You are going to hear four extracts: booking a table at a restaurant and choosing the starter, the main course and the wine. As you hear each section, complete the waiter's order form below.

```
┌─────────────────────────────────────────────────────────────┐
│     ▨   OAKLAND PARK HOUSE ═══════════                      │
│         RESTAURANT                                           │
│                                                             │
│                     ORDER FORM                              │
│                                                             │
│  Name: _ _ _ _ _          Day: _ _ _ _ _                   │
│                                                             │
│  No. of guests: _ _ _ _ _     Time: _ _ _ _ _              │
│                                                             │
│  Starters: _ _ _ _ _ _ _ _ _ _ _ _ _ _ _ _ _ _ _ _        │
│                                                             │
│            _ _ _ _ _ _ _ _ _ _ _ _ _ _ _ _ _ _ _ _        │
│                                                             │
│  Main courses: _ _ _ _ _ _ _ _ _ _ _ _ _ _ _ _ _ _        │
│                                                             │
│            _ _ _ _ _ _ _ _ _ _ _ _ _ _ _ _ _ _ _ _        │
│                                                             │
│  Drinks: _ _ _ _ _ _ _ _ _ _ _ _ _ _ _ _ _ _ _ _ _        │
└─────────────────────────────────────────────────────────────┘
```

1.2 Dilemma

Now listen to the fourth dialogue.

1. How would you react?
2. It is often said that the British are very slow to complain. They don't like causing a scene. How do people behave in your country?

---

2. Presentation

2.1 Booking a table

	How many?	*When?*
I'd like to book a table	*for* two/three/four	*for* Saturday *at* 8 o'clock

2.2 Arriving in the restaurant

	How many?	*Name?*
We've a table booked	*for* four	*in the name of* Simons

2.3 Choosing the food

Asking for a recommendation

I'm afraid you'll have to recommend something.
Could you recommend something?
Do you recommend the fish/the beef/etc.?

Giving a recommendation

I'd recommend the fish.
The fish is always excellent.

Getting your guests to decide

Have you decided?
What are you going to have?
What would you like to start/as a main course/to drink?
Would you like a drink to start with?

Indicating your decision

I'll have the fish/beef/etc.   Me too
I'll try the avocado.

2.4 Complaining

Waiter, this isn't my order/I didn't order this!
Waiter, this is cold/overcooked/undercooked/off!

2.5 Enquiring about dishes and ways of cooking

What exactly is the ... ?
What is in the ... ?
How is the ... prepared?
What comes with the ... ?

3. Controlled practice

3.1

Match the questions/statements with an appropriate response.

Questions/statements   → *Responses*

1. Could you recommend something?
2. I'm afraid we're fully booked.
3. Have you booked, sir?
4. Do you recommend the snails?
5. What would you like to drink?
6. Shall we try the Bordeaux?
7. Have you decided?
8. The shark is said to be excellent.
9. Could you manage a little bit later?
10. This beef isn't cooked at all!

(a) Yes, I'll try the garlic mushrooms.
(b) Oh dear. Could you manage a little bit earlier?
(c) I think I'd like some white wine — something dry.
(d) Yes, I'd recommend the Parma ham.
(e) Well, actually, I had them last time and they weren't very good.
(f) I'm very sorry, sir. I'll see to it straight away.
(g) Yes, we've a table for six in the name of Peters.
(h) Really. I'll try that then.
(i) Yes, that sounds fine.
(j) Umm... yes we could fit you in at 7.30.

3.2

Complete these sentences:

1. I'd like to _____ a table _____ three.
2. Can you _____ the shellfish?
3. What _ _ _ _ _ like _ _ _ _ _ starter?
4. Let's _____ red.
5. What would you like _____ start _____ ?
6. How _ _ _ _ _ meat _____ ?
7. What _ _ _ _ _ with the chicken?

3.3

Arrange the following terms under the appropriate headings.

Courses   Meat   Poultry   Vegetables   Fruit   Salads   Methods of cooking

beef	pork	mushrooms	green pepper
lettuce	cucumber	turkey	cabbage
cauliflower	chicken	veal	fried
lamb	grilled	apple	pear
tomato	banana	carrots	peas
boiled	baked	potatoes	grapes
roasted	orange	grapefruit	spinach
beans	leeks	starter	main course
pineapple	asparagus	entrée	dessert

Practise ordering dishes from this list: e.g.

I'll have the roast lamb with baked potatoes for my main course.

4. Transfer

SMALL GROUP WORK

Use the menu opposite to practise choosing a meal.
One member of the group should be the host/ess, another should be the waiter/waitress and the others are the guests invited to the meal.

OAKLAND PARK HOUSE
RESTAURANT

Starters

Soup of the day
Chilled melon
Avocado and prawns
Mackerel paté

Main Courses

Smoked salmon
Chicken cordon bleu
Chilli con carne
Barbequed chicken
Vegetable pie
Beef medallions

All main dishes are served with a selection of fresh vegetables and potatoes

Desserts

Crêpes suzette
Lemon surprise pudding
Blackcurrant cheesecake
A wide choice of ice creams and sorbets
A selection of matured and fresh cheeses

UNIT 15 **Food and drink 2**

(courtesies at dinner; inviting, appreciating, apologising)

Introduction

During a meal, there are many small courtesies which should be expressed to the host/ess. This unit focuses on some typical exchanges during and at the end of a meal.

1. Listening 📼 ──────────────────────────

1.1 Information transfer

Listen to the short extracts from a dinner party. As you listen, decide what the guest's intention is, choosing from the list. Also note details of the situation. The first is done for you.

Intentions: to express thanks/appreciation
to express an apology
to express urgency
to express an invitation
to express a request

Extract 1: Intention: __ *Request.* __ *Pass salt* _____

Extract 2: Intention: _____

Extract 3: Intention: _____

Extract 4: Intention: _____

Extract 5: Intention: _____

Extract 6: Intention: _____

Extract 7: Intention: _____

1.2 Dilemma

Now listen to the eighth extract.

1. How would you react?
2. In Britain it is becoming less and less usual for friends to drop in without an invitation. What is the position in your country?

---

2. Presentation

Notice the way the guests expressed their intentions and the hostess responded.

2.1 Expressing thanks/appreciation

	Response
This is really very good.	→ I'm glad you like it.
That was delicious.	→ I'm glad you enjoyed it.
Thanks for the lovely evening.	→ I'm glad you could come.

2.2 Expressing an apology

I'm sorry, I've spilt the sauce.	→ It doesn't matter.
I'm afraid the meat is a bit overcooked.	→ It seems fine to me.
I'm sorry I'm late.	→ Never mind.
Not for me, thank you. I can't eat (meat).	→ Oh I am sorry. Can I get you something else?

2.3 Expressing a request

Could you pass the salt?	→ Of course, here you are.
Could I just use your phone?	→ Certainly, it's over there.
Could I have a glass of water?	→ Of course, I'll get one.
May I use your loo/bathroom?	→ Of course. It's just along there.

2.4 Expressing urgency

We must leave now. be on our way.	→ Really? Can't you say a little longer?
I'm afraid we have to go.	→ That's a pity.
We'd love to stay but ...	→ We understand.

2.5 Returning the invitation

You must come to dinner with us. → That would be nice.
Next time, you must come to our
place → Fine, we'd like that.

3. Controlled practice

3.1

Match the expressions on the left with the most appropriate response on the right.

1. Could you show me where the toilet is?
2. Thanks for the lovely evening.
3. Oh, I am sorry. I've spilt wine all over the carpet.
4. I'm afraid we have to leave now.
5. This tastes wonderful.
6. You must come round to eat with us soon.
7. Could you pass the sugar?
8. I'm afraid our babysitter will be wondering where we are.
9. I'm sorry, I don't eat meat.
10. Why don't you come round to eat next Wednesday?

(a) Of course, here you are.
(b) Don't worry, I'll wipe it up.
(c) I'm glad you like it.
(d) That would be nice.
(e) Certainly, just down there on the right.
(f) I'm glad you enjoyed it.
(g) I understand. We always have the same problem.
(h) Really? That's a pity.
(i) We'd love to, but I'm afraid we are already tied up.
(j) It doesn't matter. We've got a nice salad.

3.2

Express the following, using the words in brackets.

1. Congratulate your host/ess on the meal (*delicious*)
2. Tell your host/ess you have had a lovely evening. (*Thank you . . . enjoyable*)
3. Reassure your guest not to worry about his late arrival. (*Please don't . . . matter. Two sentences*)
4. Tell your host/ess you have to leave. (*I'm sorry . . . on my way*)
5. Tell your host/ess you would like to return the invitation. (*You must . . . soon*)
6. Apologise to your host/ess for not finishing the dish. (*Please forgive me . . . not hungry any more*)
7. Explain to your host/ess that you can't eat the mushrooms. (*Would you mind . . . ?*)
8. Apologise to your guests for putting in too much salt. (*Sorry . . . salty*)
9. Tell you friend you cannot accept her dinner invitation. (*Sorry, but . . . engagement*)
10. Ask your host/ess how he/she made a particular dish. (*Could you . . . recipe?*)

3.3

What sort of food and drink would you expect at the following occasions?

(a) a business breakfast in a hotel
(b) a picnic with your host's family
(c) a company-headquarters reception
(d) a cocktail party at an embassy
(e) a fondu
(f) a celebration dinner
(g) a finger buffet after a meeting
(h) a board meeting
(i) a cheese and wine party
(j) a garden party
(k) Christmas dinner (lunch) in England
(l) a barbecue

4. Transfer

PAIR WORK

Student A: Play the role of the guest. Practise thanking, apologising, requesting, congratulating, leaving, etc. on the occasion of a dinner party.
Student B: Play the role of host/ess.

Entertainment 2

(time and money)

Introduction

In this unit you are going to hear some recorded extracts concerned with entertainment and places of interest.

1. Listening 🔲───────────────────────────────

1.1 Information transfer

You are going to hear three extracts. As you listen, make notes below.

Extract 1

Place: Madame Tussaud's Wax Works

Opening days: _ _ _ _ _

Opening times: Monday to Friday: 9–6

                 Saturday: _ _ _ _ _

                 Sunday: _ _ _ _ _

Tickets cost: £5 adults

              _

                 Monday — free

Additional information: _ _ _ _ _ _ hours _ _ _ _ _ _ _

                               _ _ _ _ _ _ _ _ _ _ _ _ _ _ _ _

Extract 2

Place: Cactus City Wild West Theme Park

Opening months: _ _ _ _ _ _

Opening days: _ _ _ _ _ _

Opening times: *10 a.m. to sundown*

Wide West Show takes place: _ _ _ _ _ _

Performances start: _ _ _ _ _ _

Performances last: _ _ _ _ _ _

Price of admission: Adults: _ _ _ Children : _ _ Family ticket : _ _

(Wild West show: _ _ _ _ _ _ extra per _ _ _ _ _ _)

Additional information: _

Extract 3

Place: Alhambra Theatre

Event: __ __ __ __ __

Performance days: __ __ __ __ __   Matinee days: __ __ __ __ __

Performance starts: __ __ __ __ __   Matinee starts: __ __ __ __ __

Performance finishes: __ __ __ __ __   Matinee finishes: __ __ __ __ __

Tickets cost: __ __ __ __ __

Additional information: __ __ __ __ __ __ __ __ __ __   half an hour
                        before the performance starts.

1.2 Dilemma

Now listen to the fourth extract. It continues from Extract 3.

1. What would you decide to go to?
2. Imagine that you want to take some business friends out to a typical show, spectacle or event in your town or country. What would you take them to see?
3. Different cultures have different ideas about public performances. Discuss these questions in relation to popular shows, events, etc., in your culture:

    (a) At what time do shows usually begin?
    (b) How long do they last?
    (c) How do people in the audience behave? (Silently, laughing, crying, talking? Would they drink or smoke?)
    (d) How does the audience show approval or disapproval?
    (e) What do people do when the show has finished?

_____ [tape]

2. Presentation

In the listening section you heard expressions concerned with:

    time
    money and cost

Let's look at these in more detail.

2.1 Time

In the following examples, note the verbs concerned with opening, starting, finishing, closing and duration.

The museum *is open* seven days a week.
It *opens* at 9 o'clock.
Performances *start* a 2 o'clock.
The show *lasts* for two and a half hours.
It *takes* a minimum of two hours to go round the museum.
The show will *run* until the beginning of July.
The museum *closes* at 6 o'clock.
The performance *finishes* at 10.45.
The matinee *ends* at 4.45.

Note the following questions:

What time/When does the show *begin/start/finish/end*?
What time/When does the museum *open/close*?
How long does the tour *last*?

Note also these 'time' prepositions:

It opens *at* 9 o'clock. (*at* with times on the clock)
There is a matinee performance *on* Saturday. (*on* with days of the week)
There is a special matinee *on* 23 April. (*on* with dates)
The programme will change *in* May. (*in* with months)
It is open *from* 9 *to* 5. (*from* ... *to* ... for start-point and end-point)

Note: Americans say 'We're open April through September' where British people would say 'We're open from April to September inclusive'.

The show will run *until* the beginning of July. (end-point)

2.2 Money and cost

Note these words and expressions:

Tickets cost £5 for adults.
Tickets are £5 for all seats.
Tickets are available at half price half an hour before the performance.
Admission is free on Mondays.

Note the following questions:

How much are tickets?/How much is a ticket?
How much/What does a ticket cost?
What's the price of a ticket?
How much do you charge?
Are there any reductions for students?
Do you take/accept credit cards?

3. Controlled practice

3.1

John is speaking to Ann on the phone. He wants to invite her to come to the theatre. Complete the dialogue below.

JOHN: Ann, I've just got two tickets for the show 'Evita' _____ Tuesday. Would you like to go?

ANN: Oh, I'd love to. But did you say Tuesday? I've got to work late _____ 29th March.

JOHN: That's OK. Tuesday's the 28th. Anyway, the performance _ _ _ _ _ 7.30.

ANN: Lovely. So let's meet _____ 7.15.

JOHN: How about a drink before? There's a bar in the theatre which _ _ _ _ _ 6.30.

ANN: OK. Oh by the way _ _ _ _ _ _ _ _ _ _ _ _ _ _ _ _ _ _?

JOHN: About three hours. It _ _ _ _ _ _ 10.20. We could have something to eat afterwards. There's a nice Italian restaurant near the theatre which _ _ _ _ _ till midnight.

ANN: That sounds nice. And _ _ _ _ _ _ the tickets?

JOHN: Oh, let's not talk about money now. It's an invitation.

ANN: Well, we can argue about that later. Anyway, I'll see you _____ Tuesday _____ 6.30, in the bar.

74

3.2

Match the questions on the left with the most appropriate answer on the right.

1. When does the match begin?
2. How much is it to get in?
3. How long does the performance last?
4. Is there any reduction for large groups?
5. Do you accept credit cards?
6. When does the bar open?
7. What time does the restaurant close?
8. Are there any tickets still available for the show tonight?
9. Where can we buy tickets?
10. Is there a charge for admission?

(a) I'm afraid not. Tickets are completely sold out.
(b) Yes. We can offer a discount of 20 per cent if there are more than ten of you.
(c) About two and a half hours.
(d) At 5 o'clock. The 'happy hour' is from 5 till 6, with drinks at half price.
(e) Not if you're a club member. Members are admitted free.
(f) The kick-off is at 7.30.
(g) Last orders are at 11.30, but diners are welcome to stay for another hour.
(h) £4 for adults and £2 for children.
(i) You can pay by Visa or American Express.
(j) They're on sale at the box office.

3.3

Look at these uses of the words *cost, charge* and *price*:

A meal in Maxims will cost you £40. (*cost* is a verb)
The cost of the meal was £10. (*cost* is a noun = money you pay for *doing* something or obtaining a *service*)
The price of computers is going down all the time. (*price* is a noun = the money you pay for particular *objects*)
The car company charged me £50 for repairing my car. (*charge* is a verb)
There will be a small charge for admission to the ground. (*charge* is a noun = money you pay to be *allowed* to do something)

Use *cost, charge* or *price* to complete the sentences below. Make tense changes and add endings if necessary.

1. I won't _____ you anything for these books — you can have them for nothing.
2. When I look at the _____ in the shops they always seem to be getting higher.
3. The _____ of living is very high in Norway and Sweden.
4. If you are a guest in the Atlantic Hotel there is no extra _____ for the use of the sports equipment.
5. 'How much did that jacket _____ you?' 'Only £20 — isn't it cheap?'
6. I got a good _____ for the car I sold.

7. The _____ of a taxi to the airport is around £12.
8. It _____ more than £5 to get a good haircut nowadays.
9. If you have goods that people want, you can _____ a high _____ for them.
10. There was a _____ of $40 just to get into the nightclub — and that didn't include drinks.

4. Transfer

PAIR WORK

Student B: Turn to the Key Section.
Student A: You work in the Tourist Information Office in your town. Think of three events that are taking place this week. They can include:

> a sporting event (e.g. a football match)
> a concert (e.g. by a pop singer or pop group)
> another event of your choice

Decide on the times and places of the events, the price of tickets, and so on. Be ready to answer Student B's questions.

GROUP WORK

Design a poster for the kind of event/entertainment which interests people in your group. Discuss the time, place, price of tickets and so on. Draw the poster and pin it on the wall.

Telephoning

(phone language)

Introduction

In this unit you are going to hear some telephone calls which show the language used by callers, people called and switchboard operators.

1. Listening 📼

1.1 Information transfer

Listen to three telephone calls. Fill in the notes below.

	Call 1	Call 2	Call 3
Caller's name: _	?		?
Company or institution taking the call: _			
Caller wants to speak to: _			
Is the call connected immediately? (*yes/no*) _ _ _ _ _ _ _ _ _ _ _ _ _ _ _ _ _		No	
Is the result: S = 'successful', E = 'engaged', NR = 'no reply'? _			
Does the caller leave a message? (*yes/no*) _			

1.2 Dilemma

Now listen to another telephone conversation.

1. What would you do if you were making the call? What would you do if you were Mr Marco and you knew there was a call for you?
2. In different cultures there are different ideas about allowing interruptions by telephone callers while you are busy with other things (meetings, etc.). What is the situation in your culture? Are you expected to break off your business to take telephone calls?
3. In Britain the phone is the most common way for friends (even neighbours) to stay in touch. How important is the phone in your country?

2. Presentation

Look at phrases which may be used by the caller, the switchboard operator and the person called.

2.1 Phrases used by the caller

Can I speak to (Mr Brown), please?
Hello, *is that* (Mr Brown)?
My name is (Chris White). (first introduction)
This is (Chris White). (subsequent introduction)
I'm ringing to find out if you can ...
I'm phoning to ask if you have ...
Could you give (him) a message, please?
Could you ask (him) *to* phone me at (number)?
Could you tell (him) I called, please?
Thanks very much. Bye.

2.2 Phrases used by the switchboard operator

When answering the phone: Good morning/afternoon. (name of company).
                          May I help you?/Can I help you?
On hearing the name of the person called: Hold the line, please.
                          I'll put you through.
When the number starts ringing: It's ringing for you now.

If the person called doesn't answer: I'm sorry. There's no reply.
I'm sorry. I'm not getting any reply.
If the person called is using the telephone: I'm sorry, the number is engaged/busy
(American English). Do you want to
hold?
Offering to take a message: Would you like to leave a message?
Can I take a message?
Can I give (him) a message?
Offering to arrange a return call: Shall I ask (him) to call you back?

2.3 Phrases used by the person called

Hello. (number).
Hello. John Brown speaking.
Speaking.

3. Controlled practice

3.1

Write numbers at the end of the sentences to show the correct order. At the
beginning of the sentences write in C (= caller), O (= operator) or P (= person
called)

_____ : Just a moment please. I'll put you through. ( )

_____ : Good morning. IBF Electronics. ( )

_____ : Hello Louise. This is George Brandt. I wanted to thank you
for the report you sent us. ( )

_____ : Ringing for you now. ( )

_____ : Hello, Louise Blanc speaking. ( )

_____ : Hello, could I speak to Miss Louise Blanc, please? ( )

3.2

What would the people say in the situations below? Write suitable sentences below. It may not be necessary to include all the information given. Add any phrases you wish in order to make the conversation more natural.

1. The switchboard operator at Esperanza College answers the telephone. The time is 9.30 a.m.

   _____

2. Mr Sigmund Hertz wants to speak to the Director of Studies.

   _____

3. The operator promises to make the connection.

   _____

4. The operator tells Mr Hertz that the number he wants is ringing.

   _____

5. The Director of Studies, Ms Maria Primo, answers the telephone.

   _____

6. Mr Hertz introduces himself and asks if the results of the English examination have arrived yet.

   _____

7. Ms Primo says that she is expecting them to arrive later today.

   _____

Now finish the conversation:

_____

_____

_____

3.3

Look at some words and expressions relating to telephone calls.
(*Note*: Both British and American forms are given, as both forms may be used internationally.)

a local call
a long-distance call
a transfer-charge call (= *collect call*, Am.E.)
a personal call

area code
phone book/telephone directory (= *telephone book*, Am.E.)
Directory Enquiries (= *Directory Assistance*, Am.E.)

Now test yourself to see if you know the meaning of these words. Complete the sentences below with the appropriate British English forms.

1. 'Do you know Joe Brown's number?' 'No, but you can look it up in the
   _ _ _ _ _.'

2. Hello, operator. I'd like to make a _ _ _ _ _ to Miss Mary White in Hong Kong. The number is Hong Kong 7227259.

3. 'I don't know Jim's new number — he's just moved house.' 'Well you could get his new number from _ _ _ _ _.'

4. _ _ _ _ _ are usually much more expensive than _ _ _ _ _

5. 'What's the _ _ _ _ _ for Edinburgh?' 'I think it's 031.'

6. 'I haven't got any money to pay for a call to my father.' 'Well, you can make a _ _ _ _ _ — that means that he pays for the call.'

4. Transfer

PAIR WORK

Student B: Turn to the Key Section.
Student A: You want to speak to Mrs Joan Bell, Managing Director of Delifoods, to arrange a meeting. Call Delifoods and ask the operator (Student B) to put you through.

GROUP WORK

Work with two other students. Students B and C turn to the Key Section.

Student A: You represent a company that sells cosmetics. You want to speak to the Assistant Manager of Beauty Stores to arrange a time when you can come and talk about your goods and prices. You would like to arrange a meeting for the day after tomorrow. You are not free on any other day this week. The time now is 14.30.

Handling the language

(clarifying, checking and monitoring)

Introduction

In this unit you are going to hear some of the ways in which listeners show that they understand, check that they understand and ask for the message to be clarified.

1. Listening 🔲 ────────────────────────────

1.1 Information transfer

Listen to the first five dialogues. If you think the person has understood the information or question, tick the box (✔). If you think the person has not understood, put a cross (X). Write beside it the situation or the purpose of the conversation.

Dialogue   Purpose (suggested answers)

1		— —
2		— —
3		— —
4		— —
5		— —

1.2 Dilemma

Now listen to the sixth dialogue.

1. When you do not understand a question, or instructions, or a joke in your own language, how do you react? Do you behave differently when speaking English?
2. Discuss situations where you find it difficult to understand English. What kinds of situations are they? What kind of English causes difficulties? How can you deal with these situations?

─────────────────────────────────────── 🔲

2. Presentation

When we listen to someone we usually aren't 'passive' — we take an active part in the dialogue. We 'monitor' the message, show that we understand or don't understand and try to ensure that the message is clear to us. Here are some of the things we do, with examples from dialogues.

2.1 To show that we understand

Yes
Mm
I see
I understand

2.2 To ask the person to repeat

Sorry? (with rising intonation)
What did you say?
Could you repeat that please?

2.3 To ask for help in other ways

Can you write that down please?

2.4 To check that we have picked up the correct word

('AGM') did you say?
('Return?') (simply repeating the word or phrase)
Before the what?

2.5 To ask for clarification of an acronym

What does AGM stand for?
What does BBC stand for?

2.6 To explain the problem

I'm sorry, my English isn't very good.

3. Controlled practice

3.1

When someone does not understand, the speaker will often rephrase the message.
  Here are some ways of rephrasing the information in the dialogues in section
1. Listen to the dialogues again and match them with the sentences below.
Sometimes there is more than one sentence for each dialogue.

Dialogue number

One way, or there and back? ☐

I'll meet you at your hotel a little later. ☐

We'll try to leave early, if you don't mind. ☐

Do you really understand? ☐

It will be at about 8 o'clock. ☐

We needn't stay for the meeting. ☐

What country are you from? ☐

I'll meet you, and then take you in my car. ☐

Take a taxi. ☐

3.2

Complete the exchanges below. Use the expressions in 2.1 above.

1. A: And of course, you'll need a cross-head screwdriver for this job.

    B: _____? What kind of screwdriver?

    A: A cross-head screwdriver — one with a cross on the top of it.

2. A: ... and he's the Managing Director of the company.

    B: _ _ _ _ _, did you say?

    C: Oh yes — he's a Very Important Person.

84

3. A: Or you could put your money into our Super Saver Account at a guaranteed rate of interest of 2 per cent above the normal rate.

   B: I'm sorry, —?

   A: Oh, sorry. Look, here's a leaflet. It tells you everything. You see? 'Super Saver Account. Two per cent above the normal rate ...'

4. A: So there's this man who goes to market, and he wants to buy a horse, so he goes up to the dealer ...

   B: _____ ?

   A: That's right — the man who's selling the horses. So he goes to him and ...

5. A: So you go along Liberation Street ...

   B: _____

   A: And you turn left at the second set of traffic lights ...

   B: _____

   A: And you'll see it straight ahead of you.

   B: OK. I've got it.

6. A: Beat the eggs, add a little milk and a pinch of salt and pour the mixture into the pan.

   B: Sorry, —?

   A: Yes, of course. Beat the eggs, add a little milk and a pinch of salt and pour the mixture into the pan.

3.3

Look at some more phrases which *ask for help* or *explain the problem*.

Can you speak a little more slowly?
Can you show it to me (on the map)?
Could you explain (this sentence), please?
I'm sorry, I didn't quite catch (the last word).
I'm afraid I can't read English very well.

   Use each phrase once in the sentences below:

1. I don't understand this sentence. — — — — — — ?

2. — — — — — —. What's this word here?

85

3. I have to take the underground to Marble Arch. __ __ __ __ __ ?

4. Please, not so fast! __ __ __ __ __ ?

5. A: Do you believe in precognition?
   B: __ __ __ __ __
   A: Precognition. Do you believe in it?

4. Transfer

PAIR WORK

Student A: Tell your partner a joke or story.
or
Tell your partner something about life in your country, region or town.
or
Tell your partner how to do something (e.g. find a certain place, use a machine, cook something, look after some financial or business matter, follow some procedure in your school or college).

Student B: Listen, ask questions and do everything necessary to understand what your partner is saying.

Note
This can also be done in groups. One person addresses the group. Other students ask questions, check that they have understood, etc.

Weather

(scale of likelihood)

Introduction

In this unit you are going to hear seven short forecasts of the weekend weather around Europe.

1. Listening

1.1 Information transfer

First look at the symbols for the different weather conditions. Then listen to the weather forecasts for the weekend. As you listen, indicate which country will have the weather conditions shown.

Weather conditions	Country/region
Sunny	_ _ _ _ _
Fair	_ _ _ _ _
Cloudy	_ _ _ _ _
Rain	_ _ _ _ _
Snow	_ _ _ _ _
Cold and clear	_ _ _ _ _
Windy	_ _ _ _ _

1.2 Dilemma

Now listen to the short dialogue.

1. How would you react?
2. In Britain the weather is a very popular topic of conversation. Is it popular in your country?

---- | ⊙⊙ |

2. Presentation

In the weather forecasts the presenter indicated different degrees of likelihood, as follows:

describing what will *certainly* happen
describing what will *probably* happen
describing what may *possibly* happen
describing what will *probably not* happen
describing what will *certainly not* happen

Now let's look at the language used in greater detail.

2.1 Describing what will *certainly* happen

The weather *will definitely* remain grey and cloudy.
The weather this weekend *will certainly* improve.

2.2 Describing what will *probably* happen

By Monday the weather *is likely to* improve.
It is likely that some of you will have a little sunshine.
Temperatures *should* reach 20 degrees centigrade.

2.3 Describing what may *possibly* happen

You *may* get some very heavy outbreaks of rain.
Gusts *might* even reach 90 miles an hour.

2.4 Describing what will *probably not* happen

This *is unlikely to* last beyond Monday evening.

2.5 Describing what will *certainly not* happen

Rain *certainly won't* reach the region until the beginning of next week.

Notes
'Likely' can be used in two constructions:

with an impersonal construction: i.e. *it is likely that* ...
with a personal construction: i.e. *someone/something is likely to* ...

'May ' indicates a slightly stronger possibility than 'might'.

3. Controlled practice

3.1

The table below shows the weather forecast for different regions of Europe. Use the notes given and the scale of likelihood indicated to make sentences.

	Certainly	Probably	Possibly	Probably not	Certainly not
1. In Italy/rain/fall/in morning		✔			
2. In Spain/ temperatures/ reach/30 degrees			✔		
3. In Sweden/snow/ fall all weekend				✔	
4. In Norway/winds/ die down	✔				
5. In England/fog patches/form			✔		
6. In France/drivers/ face icy roads			✔		
7. In Switzerland/the weather/grey and cold			✔		
8. In Austria/snow/ melt/before afternoon					✔
9. In Greece/ thunderstorms/ develop/in evening	✔				
10. In Germany/snow/ stop				✔	

1. In Italy it is likely that rain will fall in the morning.

   In Italy rain is likely to fall in the morning.

2. _

3. _

4. _

5. _

6. _

7. _

8. _

9. _

10. _

3.2

The weather is a popular topic of conversation. It is polite to agree with a comment and add your own comments, using a different expression. Here are some typical expressions:

Hot weather
Phew! It's scorching!
Hot, isn't it?
Nice and warm today!

Cold weather
Chilly, isn't it? (quite cold)
It's freezing! (very cold)
It's a bit fresh today. (not very cold)

Windy
It's blowing a gale out there! (very windy)
I was nearly blown over! (very windy)
Nice, fresh breeze! (not very windy)

Wet
I got soaked!
It's so damp. (wet atmosphere)
It's tipping it down out there. (very heavy rain)
It's only a shower. (raining for a short time)
It's pouring with rain. (heavy rain)

General
It's very close, isn't it? (hot, humid, airless)
Lovely day today!
What a beautiful morning!
Better than yesterday, don't you think?
Better day today, isn't it?
Miserable weather!
Rather dull today. (cloudy, dark)

3.3

Complete these short dialogues about the weather. Then continue in the same way with a partner.

1. A: It's tipping it down out there!

    B: Yes, I _ _ _ _ _ this morning

2. A: Rather dull today!

    B: Yes, _ _ _ _ _ !

3. A: Lovely day today!

    B: Hmmm. _ _ _ _ _

4. A: Chilly, isn't it?

    B: Chilly? It's absolutely _____ !

5. A: Hot, isn't it?

    B: Yes, _ _ _ _ _ !

4. Transfer

Student B: Turn to the Key Section.

Student A: You are on a visit to the United Kingdom. Tomorrow you want to travel up to Leeds in the North of England. The weather has been very bad, and you don't know if it will be possible to travel up from London. Ring up a travel information office (Student B) and ask about:

> travel by air
> travel by rail
> travel by car
> travel by bus

Make notes on the notepad below:

NOTES

Public announcements

(passive forms)

Introduction

In this unit you are going to hear some public announcements connected with different types of travel.

1. Listening ⟨oo⟩ ————————————————————

1.1 Information transfer

First look at the tables below. Then listen to the announcements. As you listen complete the information that is missing.

Announcement 1

Departures

Destination	Flight	Departure	Gate	Notes
Delhi	BA135	10.00	27	Delayed till 11.00
Karachi	BA147	10.10	32	Now boarding
_ _ _ _ _	_ _ _ _ _	10.30		_ _ _ _ _
Nassau	BA233	11.00	11	Go to gate
Pittsburg	BA217	11.45		

Announcement 2

POL CHICHUGU

GOVERNMENT OF ROTONGA

OFFICIAL PASSPORT

029988 LR

VALIDITY   *VALIDITE*

This passport is valid for all countries unless otherwise
endorsed (subject to any visa or other entry regulations
of countries to be visited)
Ce passeport est valable pour tous pays, sauf mention
spéciale (sous réserve des formalités de visas ou autres
réglements d'entrée des divers pays)

This passport expires   Ce passeport expire le

11 MAR 1998

unless extended   à moins de prolongation

Issued at   Délivré à

PASSPORT OFFICE
11 MAR 1988
145
ROTONGA

Date   Date

LANDING CARD

Please complete clearly in BLOCK CAPITALS

Family name: ....

Forename: ....

Passport number: ....

Issued on: ....

Issued at: ....

Valid till: ....

Flight number: ....

Visa number: ....

Validity: ....

Signature: ....

Announcement 3

TRAIN DEPARTURES

Destination	Departure time	Platform	Notes
York	_ _ _ _ _	_ _ _ _ _	_ _ _ _ _
York	_ _ _ _ _	_ _ _ _ _	_ _ _ _ _

Announcement 4

Buffet open from _ _ _ _ _ _ to _ _ _ _ _ _
Food and drink available:
Tea   ✓
Coffee
Beer
Lager
Other alcoholic drinks
Cold sandwiches

1.2 Dilemma

Now listen to the fifth announcement.

1. It is now 15.00 and you have a meeting in Barona tomorrow at 09.00. Do you use one of the other forms of transport offered or cancel the appointment?
2. Sometimes you have no alternative but to cancel an appointment; at other times it is simply convenient. How do you feel if you have to cancel an appointment? How do you feel if someone else has to cancel an appointment with you?

2. Presentation

In the announcements you heard a number of passive verb forms. The passive is often used in official statements to make them sound more formal and authoritative.

Now let's look at the passive forms in more detail.

2.1 Present passive

The train *is expected* to arrive in 30 minutes' time.
Passengers *are invited* to proceed to the restaurant.

2.2 Past passive

On take-off I *was informed* that the radar equipment developed technical problems earlier this morning.
Because of industrial action some items of food and drink *were not delivered* to this train.

2.3 Present perfect passive

Flight BA001 to New York *has been delayed*.
Some of this evening's trains *have been cancelled* or delayed.

2.4 Passives with *will* and modal forms

These *will be collected* in a few minutes.
Further information *can be obtained* from rail staff.

2.5 Formation of passives

The passive in the simple tenses is composed of two parts:
the appropriate part of 'to be' + the past participle.
The passive after *will* and modal forms is composed of:
will or modal form + 'be' + the past participle.

3. Controlled practice

3.1

Make announcements by linking a sentence from the upper list (1–5) with one from the lower list (a–e). In each case start with a sentence from the upper list and write the letter of the following sentence in the brackets.

1. We are preparing for take-off. ( )
2. We have just landed at London Heathrow airport. ( )
3. We regret to announce a delay of about one hour. ( )
4. Final call for flight BA079. ( )
5. In a few minutes we will be handing out landing cards. ( )

(a) Passengers are invited to proceed to the restaurant.
(b) Any passenger not holding an EC passport is required to complete one before disembarkation.
(c) Passengers are requested to fasten their seat belts.
(d) Any remaining passengers are urgently requested to go to gate 7 immediately.
(e) Passengers are reminded to remain in their seats until the plane has come to a complete standstill.

3.2

Put the following sentences into the passive to make them less personal. The first one has been done for you.

1. You can obtain more details from the information desk.

   More details can be obtained from the information desk.

2. You must fill in this claim form now.

   _____

3. We had to change the flight schedule for technical reasons.

   _____

4. We have now corrected the fault in the equipment.

   _____

5. We expect the plane to leave at 19.30.

   _____

97

6. We delivered your luggage to the hotel this morning.

    _

7. You should place all heavy articles in the overhead lockers.

    _

8. You can take only one item of hand luggage on board.

    _

3.3

Some announcements are good news, some bad news, and some just present neutral information. Look at the announcements below and mark them with an appropriate heading, as follows:

G = 'Good news'
B = 'Bad news'
N = 'Neutral information'

1. We are pleased to inform you that ... _____
2. The buffet car is situated at the rear of the train. _____
3. We regret to announce that ... _____
4. We are happy to be able to tell you that ... _____
5. Will all passengers holding blue boarding cards please proceed to the aircraft now. _____
6. The bar will be open from 2 p.m. until 6 p.m. _____
7. We are sorry that this will cause some inconvenience. _____
8. Unfortunately this is beyond our control. _____

4. Transfer

1 GROUP WORK

Look at the following announcements. Some are written and some spoken. First discuss which are written and which spoken, and then decide where you would see these announcements.

1. Tickets, please.
2. End of season bargains.
3. Last orders, please.
4. Vacant.
5. Guests are requested to vacate their rooms by midday.
6. Please extinguish all cigarettes.
7. Mind the doors.
8. Please do not disturb.

9. Baggage should not be left unattended at any time.
10. Books may be renewed by post or phone.

2 GROUP WORK

In your group, decide on announcements (spoken or written) which would be appropriate for your English class, your school or college, or your place of work. Then:

(a) Read out the announcements.
(b) Other students try to work out the circumstances of the announcement (who would make it, where, when and why).

The announcements can be serious, or they can be humorous — for amusement only.

KEY SECTION   Units 1–20

This section contains:

  i tapescripts and keys to the listening exercises
 ii answers to the controlled-practice exercises
iii information for the transfer section where required

First meetings 1

---

1. Listening ⬚

1.1 Information transfer

Tapescript

Dialogue 1

A: First of all, I'd like to welcome you to Vienna. My name is Patricia Graham and I will be your guide. Please call me Trish. OK, I see there are seven of you here. So could I just check your names?
B: How do you do? I am James Newton and this is my wife Sarah.
A: Pleased to meet you both. I hope you enjoy your stay.

Dialogue 2

A: It's Mr Itoh, isn't it? Welcome to Vienna.
B: Thank you. It's nice to be here.
A: I hope you enjoy your stay at the Palace.
B: Oh, I'm sure I will. Thank you.

Dialogue 3

A: And you must be Mr and Mrs Ellis.
B: Yes, that is correct. May I introduce my wife Helen?
C: Nice to meet you.
A: Nice to meet you, too, Mrs Ellis. Oh, yes, Mr Ellis, you're in the Grand, aren't you?
B: Please call me George. Yes, that's right.
A: Right. OK. How many nights are you staying with us?
B: Seven.
A: Fine, thank you.

Dialogue 4

A: How do you do? My name is Lampola.
B: Hello, Mr Lampola. Pleased to meet you. Oh, by the way, I haven't got your first name. Only your initial, H.
A: Yes, it's Hari, Hari Lampola.
B: Fine, thanks, Mr Lampola. And I hope you enjoy the suite.
A: I hope so, too.

Answer to the listening task

 Tyrol Tours

Resort: *Vienna*   Representative: *Trish Graham*

Name		Length of stay	Hotel	Type of room
1. Ellis, George	✓	7 nights	The Grand	Double
2. Ellis, Helen	✓	7 nights	The Grand	Double
3. Lampola, Hari	✓	4 nights	The Casino	Suite
4. Newton, James	✓	10 nights	The Casino	Twin
5. Newton, Sarah	✓	10 nights	The Casino	Twin
6. Itoh, Keiichi	✓	7 nights	The Palace	Single

1.2   Dilemma

Tapescript

Dialogue 5

A: So, that just leaves one person.
B: Yes, how do you do? My name is Eric Jones.
A: Pleased to meet you, Mr Jones, and welcome to Vienna.
B: Thank you.
A: Well, Mr Jones, I'm very sorry, but your name isn't on my list.
B: But I booked months ago. I've got confirmation here.

3.   Controlled practice

3.1

1. Appropriate

2. Inappropriate
   A: How do you do?
   B: How do you do?
or
   A: Nice to see you. How are you?
   B: I am very well, thank you.

3. Inappropriate
   A: I am Frank Richards. Please call me Frank.
   B: Nice to meet you. My name's Annabel Pilkington-Smythe. You can call me Ann. It's much simpler.

4. Inappropriate
   A: John, nice to see you. How are you?
   B: Not too good, I'm afraid. And you?
   A; Oh, what's the problem/matter?

5. Appropriate

3.2

PAUL: How do you do, Mr Coombs? (4)
JEAN: Pleased to meet you. Mine's Jean Braun. (2)
LIZ: Well, I think we all know each other now. So what about an aperitif? (7)
PAUL: Oh, please call me Paul. (5)
LIZ: How do you do? My name is Liz White. (1)
JEAN: OK. Fine. In that case please call me Jean. (6)
LIZ: And this is Paul Coombs, a colleague from work. (3)

UNIT 2 **First meetings 2**

1. Listening 🔘

1.1 Information transfer

Tapescript

Extract 1

A: OK everybody. This will be our first encounter-group activity. I'd like each of you to say a few words about yourself to the rest of the group ... as a kind of introduction. So, Mary, would you like to start.

B: Well, my name's Mary ... Mary Wilkins. I'm 35 years old. I work as a secretary in an insurance company. I'm divorced ... I got divorced three years ago. And I've got two children. I'm here because I'm having difficulties ...

Extract 2

Good evening. I am Paul Roberts. I am a solicitor ... in fact I am one of five partners in the company. So I'm self-employed. I specialise in company law. Well, that's the professional side. In my spare time I like the theatre and classical music ... and to be with friends. I'm a bachelor. But my friends say it's never too late. So the reason I'm here is because ...

Extract 3

Hello. I'm George Evans. I won't tell you my age ... but I can see I am the oldest here. I retired five years ago after 40 years in the theatre. First I worked as an actor and then as a director. I've got three grown-up children. They have all left home now ... and my wife died last year. But I am still healthy and quite active. I play tennis and golf. I like travelling and go abroad at least once a year. But I find that my life ...

Extract 4

Hi. My name is Susanne ... Susanne Richards. But please call me Sue. I work for General Pharma, the big chemical company just outside town. I'm on the technical side ... in R and D ... sorry! research and development. I work as a research assistant. I'm single. That's about all. And that's really why I wanted to ...

Answer to the listening task

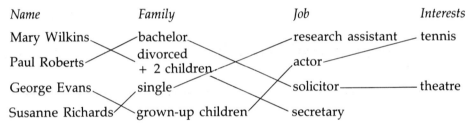

Name	Family	Job	Interests
Mary Wilkins	bachelor	research assistant	tennis
Paul Roberts	divorced + 2 children	actor	
George Evans	single	solicitor	theatre
Susanne Richards	grown-up children	secretary	

1.2 Dilemma

Tapescript

Extract 5

Good evening. My name is John Kirkpatrick. My problem is I'm very shy.

3. Controlled practice

3.1

1. Hello. My name is Allan. I'm *single*. I *work as* a teacher *in* a primary school.

2. Good evening. I'm Geraldine. Please call me Gerry. I'm *divorced*. I've *got* two children. I *am* the Marketing Manager *for* a fashion magazine.
3. Hello. My name is Lesley. I *am married*. I've *got* three children. I *work/am in* computers.

3.2

1. d	6. i
2. e	7. a
3. h	8. c
4. j	9. g
5. b	10. f

UNIT 3 **Things in common**

1. Listening 🔘

1.1 Information transfer

Tapescript

Dialogue 1

(In a hotel bar)

A: Hello. My name's Harry Duval. I'm from England.
B: OK.
A: Are you here on holiday?
B: Yes.
A: Are you staying long?
B: No. Bye.

Dialogue 2

(In an airport departure lounge)

A: Hello. Where are you travelling to?
B: I'm off to Paris for the weekend.
A: Oh, Paris is wonderful at this time of year.
B: And where are you off to?
A: We're going to Madrid.
B: Oh, Madrid is one of my favourite cities.
A: So you've obviously been there.
B: Mmm, yes. Have you been there before?

A: Yes, we were there two years ago.
B: Well, then I'm sure you visited the Prado ...

Dialogue 3

(At a party)

A: Hello. I'm Sandy. I don't seem to know anybody here.
B: No, I don't either.
A: Are you a friend of Hugh's?
B: Hugh?
A: Hugh, the host. That's him over there.
B: No, not really.
A: Then you must know Sue.
B: Sue?
A: Yes, his wife Sue.
B: No, don't think so.

Dialogue 4

(In a bus)

A: Nice day.
B: Yes, isn't it.
A: Can't remember the last time it was so nice.
B: 1984. We had a good summer in 1984.
A: Yes, that's right. I remember it now because we went abroad and it rained.
B: Oh, what a pity.
A: Yes, it certainly was. Cost us a fortune — for two weeks of rain.
B: So where did you go?
A: We took a package holiday to ...

Answer to the listening task

Dialogue 1   Type 1
Dialogue 2   Type 2
Dialogue 3   Type 1
Dialogue 4   Type 2

1.2 Dilemma

Tapescript

Dialogue 5

(In a hotel)

A: Hello, George. This is a coincidence! What are you doing here.
B: I'm here for our annual sales conference, Peter.

A: Of course, you work for Grabbit and Wrun now. You must be earning a lot of money these days.

_____ 오오

3. Controlled practice

3.1

1. *Where are you off to?*
   We're off to Amsterdam.

2. *Do you enjoy/like playing* tennis?
   Yes, very much. In fact I play at least once a week.

3. *Where do you come from?*
   Well, I was born in England, but now I live in California.

4. *Have you ever been to* Japan?
   Not yet. But I hope to get there one day.

5. So *what do you do?*
   Well, actually I'm retired now.

6. *Whew, it's hot today,* isn't it?
   Absolutely boiling!

7. *So what do you do in your spare time?*
   In fact I don't have much spare time.

8. So *what's your line of business?*
   Line of business? Well, I'm a brain surgeon.

3.2

1. a
2. b
3. c
4. a
5. b

3.3

Would you mind if I asked how much you earn? (M)
I don't want to be inquisitive, but do you belong to a party? (P)
Forgive me for asking, but could you tell me your age? (A)
Are you by any chance a member of the church? (R)
How are things at the moment? (H)

How old are you, if you don't mind my asking? (A)

That's a beautiful dress. It must have cost the earth. (M)

I've often wondered about the troubles in your country. How is the situation at present? (P)

Excuse me for asking, but that medallion is the patron saint of travellers, isn't it? (R)

I heard that you weren't too well. I hope things are better now. (H)

3.4

Suggested answers

1. It sounds awfully rude to ask, but how old is your husband?
2. I hope you don't mind my asking, but is your job well paid?
3. Don't be offended, but what do you think of your president?
4. It sounds awfully rude to ask, but are you ill? You look terrible.
5. Would you mind telling me if you are married to that man?

UNIT 4 Origins 1

1. Listening 📼

1.1 Information transfer

Tapescript

Dialogue 1

A: Where do you come from?

B: I'm from Lille — it's in the North of France.

A: Oh. Is it near Paris?

B: Not so far. It's a big industrial city but much smaller than Paris. What about you?

A: I'm from Seville.

B: Oh yes, in the South of Spain.

A: That's right. It's one of the biggest towns in the South.

Dialogue 2

A: Where are you from?
B: A place called York, it's in the North of England.
A: I'm afraid I've never been to the North. What's it like?
B: Very beautiful. York's one of the most interesting cities in the country.
A: Really? More interesting than Oxford or Cambridge?
B: Yes, I'd say so.

Dialogue 3

A: I'm from Padua.
B: Whereabouts is that?
A: Well, it's not so far from Venice.
B: I'm afraid I've only been to Milan in Italy.
A: I see. Padua's much smaller than Milan but much more attractive.
B: Oh well, next time I'll have to visit it.

Answer to the listening task

Dialogue	Place of origin	Region	Compared with
1	Lille Seville	North of France South of Spain	Paris Other towns in South of Spain
2	York	North of England	Oxford and Cambridge
3	Padua	Near Venice	Milan

1.2 Dilemma

Tapescript

Dialogue 4

A: Where do you come from?
B: That's difficult to say.
A: What do you mean?
B: Well, I don't really come from anywhere.
A: I don't understand. You must come from somewhere?
B: No, not really. I was born in Hong Kong but since then I've lived in many countries.

3. Controlled practice

3.1

Noun	Adjective	Opposite adjective
Size	big	small
Beauty	beautiful	ugly
Age	old	new
Noise	noisy/loud	quiet
Industry	industrial	non-industrial/rural
Interest	interesting	boring
Proximity (to sea, etc.)	near	far

3.2

1. Marbella is on the South coast of Spain. It's one of *the most attractive* towns on this coast.
2. I come from Dortmund. It's an industrial city in the North of Germany. It's much *noisier* than this little village.
3. I live in York. It's much *older* than New York.
4. I'm from a village near Edinburgh. It's much *more boring* than living in the city.
5. He's from Boston. It's much *nearer* to New York than Washington.
6. We come from Cairo. It's the *biggest* city in Egypt.

3.3 Expressing location

1. I come from Stevenage; it's *to the North of* London
2. I live in Bristol; it's *by the* sea, *to the West of* London
3. I come from Aberdeen; it's *on the* coast, *to the North of* Edinburgh.
4. I don't live in a town; I live *in the country*.
5. I come from Hastings; it's *by the* sea, *in the South of* England.
6. My parents come from Belfast; it's *in* Northern Ireland.

---

1. Listening 🔘 ────────────────────────────────

1.1 Information transfer

Tapescript

Dialogue 1

A: Do you live in town?
B: No, we live outside, in the country.
A: In a village?
B: No, it's miles from anywhere; in the middle of the countryside.
A: Oh I see, what sort of place is it?
B: Well, it's an old farmhouse.
A: That sounds nice.
B: Yes it is; but it's a lot of work.

Dialogue 2

A: We've just bought a new flat.
B: Oh really. Whereabouts?
A: Well it's very convenient, right in the centre of town on the river.
B: So, have you moved in?
A: No, not yet, we've got to do some work on it. Knock through a couple of
     walls. You know the sort of thing!
B: Yes I do. Best of luck!

Dialogue 3

A: It's a detached house on the outside of town.
B: Have you got any garden?
A: Yes, we have a bit at the front and quite a large area at the back.
B: That'll keep you busy.
A: Yes, we thought we'd build a conservatory onto the back of the house.

Answer to the listening task

Dialogue: 2 Features: new, town centre, some work to do on it.

Dialogue: 1 Features: middle of countryside, old.

Dialogue: 3 Features: detached, outside town, small front garden, large back
                        garden

1.2 Dilemma

Tapescript

Dialogue 4

A: How big is your flat?
B: I've no idea. We've got a couple of bedrooms, kitchen, bath ...
A: Yes, but surely you know how many square metres it is?
B: I'm sorry. I really don't know.
A: That's strange ... Your rent must be based on that ...

---

3. Controlled practice

3.1

1. My office is *on* the third floor *at* the back of the building.
2. It's a bit noisy because it's right *on* the railway line.
3. We live just *outside* town. It takes us ten minutes to get *into* the centre.
4. The man who lives *above* me plays the drums. I can hear the sound coming *through* the ceiling.
5. We're flying *to* Greece and we'll be staying *on* one of the islands.
6. There is a shed *at* the top of the garden.
7. He lives *on* the coast and can see *across* the channel on a fine day.
8. The building is *on* the corner *at* the end of the street.

UNIT 6 **The day**

1. Listening

1.1 Information transfer

Tapescript

Dialogue 1

A: What time shall we meet tomorrow?
B: Well, I normally start at 8. What about 9?
A: Well, that's a bit early for me. I never get in before 9. Could we say 9.30?
B: Yes, that's fine for me.

Dialogue 2

A: What about lunch?
B: Yes, what a good idea. Goodness, it's already 1.30! You must be hungry.
A: Just a bit. In Sweden we usually break for lunch around 11.
B: Really! Sounds like breakfast time to me.

Dialogue 3

A: When can we expect him?
B: Well, let me see ... it's 9.15 now. Not before 10. His train doesn't leave till 8.
A: OK. We'd better get started. We rarely finish before 12 so if we don't want
    to run out of ...
B: I agree. What's on the agenda?

Answer to the listening task

Dialogue 1: Time of meeting: 9.30 a.m.
Dialogue 2: Time of lunch: 1.30 p.m.
Dialogue 3: Beginning time of meeting: 9.15 a.m.
             End time of meeting: 12 noon

1.2 Dilemma

Tapescript

Dialogue 4

A: It's 4.30. I'm off home.
B: Really! We usually work till at least 6. I rarely leave the office before 7.
A: Yes, I've noticed. But I'm used to starting early, a short lunch break and then
    leaving early to see my family.
B: I understand. I used to have a working day like that. I'm afraid you'll have
    to get used to our way of working here.

3. Controlled practice

3.1

Most frequent   always
                          often
                          usually
                          sometimes
                          occasionally
                          rarely
                          seldom
least frequent   never

3.2

Dialogue 1

A: When *do you* usually *get up*?
B: Oh about 7.
A: Do you want a call in the morning?
B: No, I always *wake up* before 7.

Dialogue 2

A: Are you hungry?
B: No, I rarely *eat/have* lunch.
A: Really! You mean nothing at all?
B: Yes. I never *have* the time.

Dialogue 3

A: *Does* he *live* round here?
B: No, he *doesn't*. He *lives* in Spain.
A: So why *does* he *come* here every year?
B: I'm not sure. They say he *comes/is here* for the beer!

3.3

1. I *used to live* in London. I now live in Edinburgh.
2. It's hard to get up early bit I *am getting used to* it.
3. He'll help you write the letter. He *is used to writing* letters.
4. I *used to* hate living in the country. I now rather enjoy it.
5. He doesn't like having to go to school but he *is getting used to* it.

UNIT 7 **The date**

1. Listening ⟨oo⟩ ———————————————————————————————

1.1 Information transfer

Tapescript

Call 1

A: Hello Pete, what about a round of golf sometime soon?
B: Good idea. Let me just get my diary ... I'm going to be pretty busy next week ...
A: Well, what abut a week on Saturday?
B: You mean the 4th May ... yes, I'm free in the morning.
A: Good, let's say 9.30 then, shall we?
B: Yes, 9.30 will be fine. I'll see you there.
A: Right. I'll look forward to it.
B: Me too. Bye.

Call 2

B: Ron, you know our game of golf next Saturday?
A: Yes.
B: I'm sorry, but I won't be able to make it. There's a problem over in the States and I'm flying out there tomorrow. I won't be back till Saturday afternoon.
A: That's a shame. Never mind, give me a ring when you get back.
B: I'll do that. Bye.
A: Bye.

Call 3

B: Ron, it's Pete.
A: Hi, how was your trip?
B: OK. A bit tiring.
A: I'm sure. So what about our golf?
B: Yes, that's what I was phoning about. Could you manage a round this week some time?
A: Just a moment. I'll have a look in my diary. I'm away Monday and Tuesday. Going to London Wednesday morning. Wednesday afternoon looks fine.
B: Fine, so that's Wednesday 8th. 2.30 suit you?
A: Yes, 2.30's fine. See you there.

Answer to the listening task

Call 1: Day and time fixed: Saturday 4 May, 09.30
Call 2: Reason for cancelling: Trip to the States
Call 3: Day and time fixed: Wednesday 8 May, 14.30.

117

1.2 Dilemma

Extract 4

A: I have an appointment to see Peter Martin.
B: Just a moment. I'll tell him you're here. What name shall I say?
A: Gordon Strachan.
B: Right Mr Strachan. If you'd like to take a seat ... I'm sorry Mr Strachan. Mr Martin's left the office already. What time was your appointment?
A: Well, I'm about 15 minutes late. It was at 5 o'clock.

3. Controlled practice

3.1

Note: there are other possible versions. This probably sounds most natural.

A: What *are you doing* next Saturday?
B: Oh, I don't know. I haven't decided. What about you?
A: *I'm going* to the cinema in the evening.
B: Oh, what *are you going to see*?
A: A film called 'A Fish called Wanda'.
B: Oh I'd like to see that. What time *does it start*?
A: At 8, I think. *I'll check* and give you a ring.
B: Thanks. I'll speak to you later then. Bye.
A: Bye.

3.3

A. 4   B. 2, 6   C. 5   D. 1   E. 3

4. Transfer

1. **Student B**:   Student A will phone you to arrange a meeting. Use the diary opposite to find a suitable time:

2. Student A will phone you to speak to Ron Kent. You are not sure where he is. Take a message. Make sure you note down the name of the caller accurately.

Monday: 13	*free all day.*	
Tuesday: 14	*free in morning* *afternoon meeting Bank Manager*	
Wednesday: 15	*09.30 : Dentist* *12.00 : Visit sister*	
Thursday: 16	*lunchtime : return from sister*	
Friday: 17	*14.00 : Leave for ski chalet*	

UNIT 8 Interests

1. Listening

1.1 Information transfer

Tapescript

Dialogue 1

A: What do you do in the evenings, James?

B: Well, we go out quite a lot . . . to the theatre, cinema, sometimes to eat. What about you?

A: Well, Sandra doesn't like restaurants. She reckons you can eat better at home.

B: I'm surprised. Joan and I enjoy a meal out. Especially Joan.

A: I don't mind it but I'm not too fond of all the arrangements — you know: booking it, getting dressed up. We prefer to go out when we feel like it. We both like going out to our local pub.

B: Joan hates pubs. She can't stand the smoke. I don't mind them.

Dialogue 2

P = Peter, M = Maria, G = Günther, S = Susan
P: What did you think of it, Maria?
M: I thought it was awful.
P: Really? I thought parts were rather good. The main actor was a bit weak but on the whole it wasn't too bad.
M: I couldn't disagree more. The whole thing was a disgrace. What did you think Günther?
G: I enjoyed it tremendously. I thought the set was marvellous and the acting very realistic. Don't you agree Susan?
S: What? Oh, it was all right . . .

Answers to the listening task

Dialogue 1

Subject	James	Joan	Ron	Sandra
Restaurants	✔	✔✔	0	X
Pubs	0	X	✔	✔

Dialogue 2

Subject	Maria	Peter	Günther	Susan
Play:	X	✔	✔✔	0

1.2 Dilemma

Tapescript

Dialogue 3

A: That was lovely!
B: Oh, I'm glad you liked it. You must have some more.
A: Well actually I'm rather full.
B: Oh go on. Surely you could manage a bit more?

3. Controlled practice

3.1 Suggested answers

1. A: Do you enjoy watching TV?
   B: *I don't mind it (watching TV)* sometimes.
2. A: What did you think of the film?
   B: *(I thought) it was tremendous/etc.*
3. A: What do you think of sport on TV?
   B: Oh, *I can't stand it/hate it/* etc.
4. A: What did you think of the meal?
   B: *It was delicious.*
5. A: What's your favourite hobby?
   B: *I'm keen on/enjoy/like* sailing.
6. A: What did you think of the wine?
   B: *It was okay/all right.*
7. A: What do you think of English food?
   B: *I don't like/hate/dislike/can't stand it.*
8. A: What did you think of the concert?
   B: *It was awful/terrible/etc.*
9. A: Do you like the climate here?
   B: Yes, *I enjoy/like/etc.* the summers.
10. A: I enjoyed his last book, didn't you?
    B: Well, actually, *I thought it was terrible/etc.*

3.2

(a) 10 (b) 2 (c) 1 (d) 8 (e) 6 (f) 4 (g) 3 (h) 7 (i) 9 (j) 5

4. Transfer

Handicrafts: dress-making, picture-framing, pottery
DIY: renovating
Games: chess
Outdoor: rambling
Racket sports: badminton
Ball sports: netball
Other sports: hang-gliding
Evening entertainment: opera

UNIT 9 **Entertainment 1**

---

1. Listening $\boxed{\text{oo}}$ —————————————————————

1.1 Information transfer

Tapescript

R = Robert, J = Jeremy, F = Francesca, JA = Jane
R: Well, that was interesting. How about a drink?
J: Good idea. Let me get them.
R: No, I'll get them. What would you like, Francesca?
F: Just a Perrier, please.
R: And you, Jane?
JA: Nothing for me thanks.
R: Really? What about you Jeremy?
J: I'll have a whisky, please.
R: With ice?
J: Yes please.
R: Right, a Perrier and two whiskies with ice. One with soda too.

R: It's a long interval. What about another drink?
J: These are on me. It's my round. Francesca?
F: No thanks, I haven't finished this one.
J: Jane, are you sure you won't change your mind?
JA: Oh. I'll have an orange juice, please.
J: Right. Robert, will you join me in another whisky.
R: Why not. Ice and soda in mine again, please.
J: Right, I'll be back in a minute.

Answers to listening task

Drinks order:

Person	*First round*	*Second round*
Francesca	Perrier	nothing
Jeremy	whisky and ice	whisky and ice
Jane	nothing	orange juice
Robert	whisky, ice and soda	whisky, ice and soda

1.2 Dilemma

Tapescript

A: Would you like to go to the concert on Thursday?
B: I'd love to but I'm busy that evening.

A: Peter, what about you?
C: Me too, I'm afraid.
A: George, wouldn't you like to come?

---

3. Controlled practice

3.1

1. You want to suggest a coffee break.
   How about/What about a coffee?
2. You want to offer a biscuit/piece of cake.
   Would you like a biscuit?
3. You're hungry and somebody says: 'How about lunch?'
   Good idea/That would be nice.
4. You're very busy and somebody says: 'Would you like to join me for lunch?'
   No thanks/I'm sorry, but I'm a bit busy.
5. You want to find out what your guests want to drink.
   What would you like to drink?
6. You want to find out what your guests want to eat.
   What would you like to eat?
7. You're thirsty and somebody says: 'Would you like a beer?'
   Yes please/That's a good idea.
8. Your host is offerring to buy the meal. You want to repay him for all his help.
   This one is on me/I'd like to pay for this.
9. Your host has bought the first round of drinks. You would like to buy the next round.
   This is my round.
10. You arrive as a guest at someone's house. You're tired and dirty. Your host says: 'Would you like a shower?'
    Yes please/That would be nice/lovely.

3.2

1. This is my round.
2. How about a drink?
3. Mine's a lager.
4. Let me get this one.

3.3

(a) I'd love to come but I really must get back to see my family.
(b) I'd love to come but I'm really very tired this evening.
(c) I'd love to come but, actually, I saw it last week.
(d) I'd love to come but I'm without my car this evening.

4. Transfer

PAIR WORK

Student B: Make offers in the following situations:
invite for dinner on Saturday
a drink after work this evening
lunch together today
another drink before you go home
join you at the rugby match on Saturday
a round of golf next week

UNIT 10 Travel 1

1. Listening 🔘

1.1 Information transfer

Tapescript

Dialogue 1

(On a bus)

A: Where do I get off for the Superstore please?
B: It is the last stop.
A: How long will it take to get there?
B: Oh, not long at this time of day. About 20 minutes.
A: OK. Thanks.

Dialogue 2

(At the railway station)

A: Which is the platform for York, please?
B: Number 4, sir.
A: Is this one going to York?
C: No, Leeds.
A: But I've just been told platform 4 for York.
C: Who told you that, sir?
A: The assistant at the information office. Anyway, which is the platform for York?
C: Platform 4B, sir.
A: And when does the next one leave?
C: At 7, sir.

124

Dialogue 3

(In the street)

A: Excuse me. Can you tell me how to get to the nearest pharmacy?
B: Well, the easiest way is by cab.
A: How much will it cost from here?
B: Oh, no more than six or seven pounds. Six-fifty, maybe.
A: Oh, that's not too bad. So, where can I get one?
B: Look there's an empty one coming now.
A: How do I stop it?
B: Just stick out your hand.

Dialogue 4

(In a travel agent's)

A: Good morning.
B: Good morning, sir.
A: I'd like to enquire about flights to Paris.
B: Yes, sir.
A: Could you tell me how often they go?
B: Let me see. The first one leaves at seven in the morning, and then there's one every hour till eight in the evening.
A: Sorry, what time does the last one leave?
B: At eight, sir.
A: Thank you.
B: Pleasure, sir.

Dialogue 5

(In a travel agent's)

B: Yes, madam.
A: My name is Anne Jenkins. I've just received my invoice for my trip to Mombasa.
B: Yes, Mrs Jenkins.
A: And I'd like to ask about the total on the invoice.
B: Yes, Mrs Jenkins.
A: I'd like to know why there is a supplement.
B: Sorry?
A: Why is there a supplement on my invoice?
B: That's because you've booked a single cabin, Mrs Jenkins. If you look at the brochure, you'll see that it says quite clearly that they charge a supplement for a single cabin.
A: OK. I see.
B: Thank you, Mrs Jenkins. Bye.
A: Good bye.

Dialogue 6

(In the tube)

A: My, this compartment's crowded.
B: Yes, I know. But if you think it's bad down here, you should see it up there.
A: I guess people will get used to anything.
B: Well, as long as it gets them from A to B. Anyway, it's much quicker than by bus or car. We're getting off at the next station: Piccadilly.
A: Er, excuse me. Do you think I could get past, please?
C: Yes, certainly.

Answers to the listening task

Dialogue	*Type of transport*	*Destination*
1	Bus	Superstore
2	Train	York
3	Taxi	Nearest pharmacy
4	Plane	Paris
5	Ship	Mombasa
6	Underground / tube	Piccadilly

1.2 Dilemma

Tapescript

Dialogue 7

(On the train)

A: Excuse me. What time do we arrive at the airport?
B: Sorry. Did you say the airport?
A: Yes.
B: This train doesn't go to the airport.
A: Oh no! My plane leaves in 90 minutes!

3. Controlled practice

3.1

Section 1

A: Good morning. Preston Travel. (1)
B: Yes, good morning. I'd like to enquire about flights to Italy. (2)
A: Yes, sir. *Where* exactly would you like to fly to? (3)
B: To Milan. (4)
A: Yes, sir, and *when* is it for? (5)
B: Out on Wednesday 12 April and back on Thursday 13. (6)
A: I see. One moment, sir. Yes, there are four flights out. (7)
B: *Where* do they leave from? (8)
A: They're from London Heathrow. (9)

Section 2

B: *What* do you have from Manchester? (10)
A: From Manchester there's just one flight a day — leaving at 8.30 in the morning. (11)
B: And *what* time does it arrive in Milan? (12)
A: 14.30. (13)
B: 14.30! *Why* does it take so long? (14)
A: Er, yes, because there's a stopover in Heathrow. (15)
B: *How* long for? (16)
A: Er, one hour. (17)
B: OK. And back? (18)
A: The return flight leaves Milan at 17.30 and arrives back in Manchester at 20.30. (19)
B: Back at 20.30. That sounds better. (20)

3.2

Suggested answers

1. Can you tell me what time the plane leaves?
2. I'd like to know where the hotel is exactly.
3. Can you tell me how much it costs?
4. I'd like to know when we visit Versailles.
5. Do you know if I have to get a visa?
6. Can you tell me if the insurance is included in the cost?
7. Can you tell me how much the cancellation fee is?
8. Do you know if the room has a private bathroom?
9. I'd like to know if there's a swimming pool.
10. Can you tell me the time difference/what the time difference is?

4. Transfer

Student B: You are planning a trip from London to Bangkok in the near future. You ring up a travel agent (Student A) to ask about flights.

Ask for the relevant information so that you can complete the details below.

Your first preference is to leave London on Sunday and arrive early on Monday by British Airways. Your second preference is to leave London on Saturday and fly via the Gulf (Bahrain or Abu Dhabi), again by British Airways.

London to Bangkok				
Days	*Depart*	*Arrive*	*Airline*	*Stops*
M./Tu./Wed./Th./Fr./Sat./Sun.				

UNIT 11 **Travel 2**

1. Listening 🔘

1.1 Information transfer

Tapescript

Dialogue 1

A: If you want to make a claim for lost luggage you'll have to fill in this form.
B: Well, I've got an appointment at 3! And I've already waited more than an hour for my luggage!
A: OK, sir. It won't take a minute. Do you mind if I ask you some questions? Then you'll just have to sign the form.
B: Not at all. Please do.

A: OK. May I ask for your full name, sir?
B: Yes. It's John Francks. That's F-R-A-N-C-K-S.
A: Thank you, sir. And where have you flown in from?
B: From Geneva.
A: The flight number? ... Can I just see your ticket?
B: Yes, of course. Here you are.
A: So, SA429 from Geneva. And the luggage ... what did it look like?
B: One black suitcase and one black travel bag — both with my name on them.
A: OK, sir. And, now, where can we contact you in London?
B: 32 Grosvenor Terrace.
A: With an S?
B: Yes, G-R-O-S-V-E-N-O-R. And that's London W2Y 4AP.
A: And do you have a contact phone number?
B: Yes, 071 437-8210.
A: Thank you, Mr Francks. We'll contact you as soon as we have any information. Oh yes. One more thing. I need to have your signature. Just here. ... Thank you.

Dialogue 2

A: Good morning, sir. Can I see your ticket, please?
B: Yes, certainly. Here you are.
A: Er, I'm afraid BA144 has been cancelled.
B: Oh no. I've got to be in Milan for a meeting at 3. I really mustn't miss that appointment.
A: Just let me check sir. ... You needn't worry, sir. There's an Alitalia flight at 11.30 that'll get you into Milan at 14.15.
B: Do you mind if I just think that over for a moment?
A: No, not at all.
B: Uh, OK, I'll take that then ... if you're sure it'll get me in on time.
A: Yes, it will.
B: OK, can I just write down the details?
A: Yes, of course, sir. It's flight AZ602.
B: Uh-huh.
A: Departing at 11.30.
B: Uh-huh.
A: And arriving at 14.15 local time.
B: OK.
A: Just one more thing. You'll have to go over to terminal 2.
B: To terminal 2?
A: There's no need to worry, sir. It'll only take a few minutes, and you've got plenty of time ...

Luggage claim

Passenger's name: John Francks

Arriving from: Geneva

Flight number: SA429

Passenger's contact address: 32 Grosvenor Terrace

London

W2Y 4AP

Contact telephone number: 071 437-8210

Delete as appropriate:

Claim for damage/loss

Description of luggage:

1. 1 black suitcase

2. 1 black travel bag

3. . . . .

Passenger's signature: ... *John Francks* . . . .

For official use only

Signature: ... *Paul Rowan* Date: *23 August 1990* . . . .

Notes

Departure time: 11.30

Arrival time: 14.15

Flight: AZ602

Departure from: Terminal 2

1.2 Dilemma

Tapescript

Dialogue 3

A: Your passport, please.
B: Here you are.
A: Sorry, sir, but where is your British visa?
B: British visa? We don't need to have a visa to visit Britain.
A: I'm afraid you do, sir. As from April 1st all citizens from your country must have a valid visa to enter this country.
B: But, I didn't have to have one two weeks ago! Really, you've got to let me in.
A: No, sir. I haven't got to let you in at all. The new regulation states that citizens from your country are not allowed to enter this country without a visa.

---

3. Controlled practice

3.1 Obligation

1. *You must have a valid visa.*
2. You *won't need to confirm your reservation.*
3. I'm sorry, but you *aren't allowed to take that bag on the plane.*
4. I *must be on the 9 o'clock flight.*
5. The direct flight was cancelled; so I *had to come via Frankfurt.*
6. I'm sorry, but you *mustn't smoke cigars here.*
7. Can I use your phone? *I've got to call the office.*
8. That's OK. You *needn't pay.*

3.2 Permission

1. c
2. e
3. b
4. a
5. d

4. Transfer

PAIR WORK

1. **Student B**: You are a sales assistant in a travel office. Student A is going to phone you to ask you if you can change his/her ticket.
   First find out what class of ticket Student A has. Is it first, club, Eurobudget, economy or APEX?
   Restrictions on APEX tickets:
   must include Saturday night stay
   dates can't be changed; can only be upgraded to club class;
   cost is £399 (an extra £200)
   If cancelled, no refunds will be made

2. **Student B**: You are the 'Baggage Claims' official at John F. Kennedy airport in New York. Student A comes up to the desk. After you are sure that the luggage has not arrived, you must fill in the following claim form. Ask questions to complete the form.

Baggage claim

Passenger's name: ....

Arriving from: ....

Flight number: ....

Passenger's contact address: ....

....

....

Contact telephone number: ....

Delete as appropriate
Claim for damage/loss

Description of baggage:

1. ....

2. ....

3. ....

Passenger's signature:...

---

1. Listening

1.1 Information transfer

Tapescript

Dialogue 1

A: What's the matter?
B: Well, I've got a bad stomach ache.
A: Um ... when did it start?
B: Yesterday morning.
A: Has it got worse?
B: Yes, it's very painful now.
A: Any other symptoms? Sickness or diarrhoea?
B: No, not really.
A: Right, let's have a look at you ... It's difficult to say. It's nothing serious. It could be something you've eaten or a bug. I'd like you to see how it goes. If it's not any better in a couple of days, come and see me again.
B: Shouldn't I take something for it?
A: No, I don't think so. You should get plenty of rest, probably best not to eat but drink plenty of fluid.

Dialogue 2

A: So, what's the problem?
B: Well, I've been getting very severe headaches recently.
A: I see. How long have you been getting them?
B: For about two weeks.
A: Have they been getting worse?
B: No, not really. They're about the same.
A: Where is the pain?
B: Right here at the front of my head.
A: I see. Any other symptoms?
B: Yes, I've been feeling sick as well.
A: Right, I'd like to examine you ... I'm not sure. It could be a sort of migraine or it may be stress. In any case I'm going to give you a prescription. I'd like you to take one of these pills two times a day. If you find they're not helping, come back and see me again.

Answer to the listening task

Patient	Illness	Duration	Other symptoms	Diagnosis	Advice/prescription
1	Stomach ache	1/2 day	None	Food or a bug	Rest, don't eat, drink a lot
2	Headaches	2 weeks	Sickness	Migraine/ stress	Pills: one twice a day

1.2 Dilemma

Tapescript

Dialogue 3

A: I've got very bad backache.
B: I'm afraid I can't do much about it. You just need to rest.
A: That's difficult. I'm here for an important meeting. Could you recommend an osteopath?
B: No, I'm not willing to do that. You know many of them haven't had any medical training.

---

3. Controlled practice

3.1 Suggested answers

I've got a stomach ache/rash/temperature.
I've got a high temperature/bloodshot eye/bad cold/swollen ankle/runny nose.
I feel sick/dizzy/faint/tired/depressed.
I've got a pain in my arm/neck/eye.

3.2

DR: What's the matter?
YOU: *I've got a pain in my chest.*
DR: How long have you had it?
YOU: *For the last two days.*
DR: Have you got any other symptoms?
YOU: No.
DR: Right, let's have a look. . . . (carries out examination) There doesn't seem to be anything serious. It *could* be a chest infection. Just in case, *I'm going to give you* a prescription. *I'd like you to take* one tablet twice a day.

Situation 2

DR: Right, what's the problem?
YOU: *I've got a fever.*
DR: When did it start?
YOU: *Three days ago.*
DR: Have you had any other symptoms?
YOU: *Yes, I've been aching all over and I've lost my appetite.*
DR: Well, it sounds as though you've got a bug. You should get plenty of rest
      and drink lots of fluid.
YOU: *Shouldn't I take something for it?*
DR: No, the best thing in these cases is to take nothing — let it run its course.

3.3

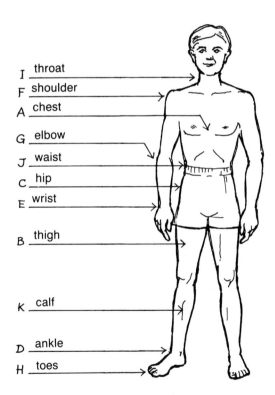

I — throat
F — shoulder
A — chest
G — elbow
J — waist
C — hip
E — wrist
B — thigh
K — calf
D — ankle
H — toes

---

1. Listening 🔊

1.1 Information transfer

Tapescript

Dialogue 1

A: Excuse me, I'm looking for an adaptor for my electric razor.
B: Yes sir, you'll find them on the first floor of the store: electrical supplies.
A: Can you help me. I'd like to buy an adaptor for my razor. It's got a continental plug on it.
C: Yes sir, we've got two types of adaptor: one multi-adaptor which can be used in any country, that's £6.85; or this one, just for the UK, that sells at £2.55.
A: I think I'll take the multi-adaptor.
C: Right sir. Anything else?
A: No, that's it. Here's a £10 note.
C: So, that'll be £6.85. . . . Thank you, and here's your change and your receipt.

Dialogue 2

A: Excuse me. I wonder if you could help me.
B: Of course sir.
A: I'm looking for a lambswool sweater for my wife.
B: Right, do you have any particular colour in mind, sir?
A: Yes, navy blue if possible.
B: Well we have two styles — one with a V-neck, one round-neck. They're the same price. Both £28.99.
A: Yes . . . that's just what I was looking for.
B: I am glad. What size please? They come in small, medium or large.
A: Small, if you've got it.
B: No problem . . . right, that'll be £28.99.
A: Do you accept Mastercard?
B: Yes sir . . . thank you . . . Right, here you are and here's your receipt.
A: Thank you very much.
B: You're welcome sir.

Answer to the listening task

Visitor	Type of shop	Item bought	Price	Method of payment
1	Store	Adaptor	£6.85	Cash
2	—	Lambswool sweater	£28.99	Credit card — Mastercard

1.2 Dilemma

Tapescript

Dialogue 3

A: I'm afraid this is too big. I'd like to have my money back.
B: Have you got your receipt?
A: Yes, here it is.
B: Thank you ... And here is your refund.

Dialogue 4

A: I'm afraid my wife doesn't like the colour. Could I have a refund?
B: I'm sorry sir. We don't give refunds unless there is something wrong with the garment.
A: Really, I thought you would always give refunds.
B: I'm afraid not sir. However, you could exchange it or we can give you a credit voucher.

---

3. Controlled practice

3.1

1. f 2. d 3. i 4. j 5. g
6. a 7. b 8. h 9. c 10. e

3.2 Suggested answers

1. *Can you tell me where* I can find a battery for my calculator?
2. I'm just *looking*, thank you.
3. I'm afraid these shoes aren't big *enough*.
4. Do you have something at a *rather more reasonable* price?
5. Could I have a *refund* please?

3.3 Suggested answers

It is too small round the chest.
It is too long in the arms.
They are too baggy round the hips.
They are too tight round the bottom.
Can I have it lengthened?
Can I have them let out?
Have you got it longer?
Have you got something in another size?
Have you got something smaller?
Have you got them in red?

3.4

(a) a kilo of beef — a butcher's
(b) a packet of cigarettes — a newsagent's
(c) a hammer — an ironmonger's
(d) half a kilo of tomatoes — a greengrocer's
(e) a suit — a men's shop
(f) a skirt — a women's shop
(g) some toothpaste — a pharmacist's
(h) some pickled olives — a delicatessen

Note
All these items could be bought in a good department store.

4. Transfer

Student B: Use the following information to help the customer:
     1. Alarm clocks are sold in the hardware department in the basement.
     2. Alarm clocks. There are three models:

       (a) traditional face clock, brass: £22.30
       (b) digital alarm clock, plastic: £9.25
       (c) digital radio—alarm clock, black plastic: £32.99

UNIT 14 Food and drink 1

1. Listening

1.1 Information transfer

Tapescript

Dialogue 1

A: Russels Restaurant.
B: I'd like to book a table for four for Saturday night at 8 o'clock.
A: I'm afraid we're fully booked at that time.
B: What if we made it a little later?
A: Well . . . we could manage 9.30.
B: That's OK.
A: What's the name please?
B: It's Simons.
A: Right, so that's a table for four, Saturday at 9.30?
B: Fine, bye.

Dialogue 2

B: I'm afraid you'll have to recommend something.
J: Well, as a starter the prawns are always very good.
B: Fine, I'll have the prawns.
J: What about you Sarah? Have you decided?
S: I think I'll have the snails. What are you going to have David?
D: I'll have an avocado.
J: Me too.

Dialogue 3

J: Right, what about main courses. The fish is always good here.
D: Umm . . . I had fish the other day. I think I'll try the pork filet.
B: Me too. Sarah, what about you?
S: I don't know. Perhaps the fish. John, do you recommend the sole?
J: Yes, it's always excellent.
S: Good, I'll have that then.
J: And I think I'll have the beef casserole.

Dialogue 4

J: Right, I'll order then. What would you like to drink with the meal. A bottle of red?

D: That sounds nice.

J: Let me just look at the wine list ... umm ... they've got a good bottle of Bordeaux. Shall we try it?

S: Yes, let's. And some mineral water. The fizzy sort.

J: OK. Waiter!

Answer to the listening task

OAKLAND PARK HOUSE RESTAURANT

ORDER FORM

Name: *Simons*   Day: *Saturday*

No. of guests: *4* _ _ _   Time: *9.30* _ _

Starters: *prawns (1), snails (1), avocado (2)*

Main courses: *pork fillet (2), sole (1), beef casserole (1)*

Drinks: *Bordeaux red, mineral water*

1.2 Dilemma

Tapescript

J = John, W = waiter, S = Sarah

J: Ah, here it is! I'm really quite hungry.
W: Yours is the beef casserole, sir?
J: Yes, that's right. You don't mind if I start? Oh no! This is disgraceful, the casserole is stone cold!
S: Really? You should send it back.

3. Controlled practice

3.1

1. d 2. b 3. g 4. e 5. c
6. i 7. a 8. h 9. j 10. f

3.2

1. I'd like to *book* a table *for* three.
2. Can you *recommend* the shellfish?
3. What *would you* like *as a* starter?
4. Let's *have* red.
5. What would you like *to* start *with* ?
6. How *do you like your* meat *done*?
7. What *is served* with the chicken?

3.3

Courses	Meat	Poultry	Vegetables
starter	beef	chicken	cauliflower
entrée	lamb	turkey	beans
main course	pork		leeks
dessert	veal		asparagus
			mushroom
			carrots
			potatoes
			green pepper
			cabbage
			peas
			spinach

Fruit	Salads	Methods of cooking
pineapple	lettuce	boiled
banana	tomato	roasted
orange	cucumber	grilled
apple		baked
grapefruit		fried
pear		
grapes		

UNIT 15 Food and drink 2

1. Listening

1.1 Information transfer

Tapescript

Extract 1

A: Could you pass the salt, please?
B: Of course, here you are.
A: Thanks.

Extract 2

A: Umm ... this meal's really very good.
B: I'm glad you like it.

Extract 3

A: Oh dear, I'm sorry. I've spilt the sauce.
B: Oh, it doesn't matter, I'll get a cloth.

Extract 4

A: Oh I am sorry, the meat's a bit overcooked.
B: It tastes fine to me.

Extract 5

A: Look at the time, we must be going!
B: Really? Wouldn't you like another coffee?
A: I'd love one, but the babysitter ...

Extract 6

A: That was a lovely meal.
B: I'm glad you enjoyed it. It was nice to see you again.

Extract 7

A: You must come round to eat at our place soon.
B: That would be nice.
A: Right, I'll give you a ring to fix a day.

Answers to the listening task

Extract 1: Intention: Request. Pass salt.
Extract 2: Intention: Thanks/appreciation. Good meal.
Extract 3: Intention: Apology. Spilt sauce.
Extract 4: Intention: Apology. Overcooked meat.
Extract 5: Intention: Urgency. Have to leave.
Extract 6: Intention: Thanks/appreciation. Lovely meal.
Extract 7: Intention: Invitation. For a meal.

1.2 Dilemma

Tapescript

Extract 8

A: Oh hello .... What a nice surprise! We're in the middle of dinner. But *do* come in.

3.   Controlled practice

3.1

1. e   2. f   3. b   4. h   5. c   6. d   7. a   8. g   9. j   10. i

3.2

1. That was a delicious meal!
2. Thank you for such an enjoyable evening.
3. Please don't worry about it. It doesn't matter.
4. I'm sorry, but I shall have to be on my way.
5. You must come and see me/us soon.
6. Please forgive me, but I find I'm not hungry any more.
7. Would you mind if I left the mushrooms?
8. Sorry the food's so salty!
9. Sorry, but I have another engagement.
10. Could you give me the recipe?

3.3

Suggested answers

(a) eggs, fruit, rolls, coffee, etc.
(b) sandwiches, salad, fruit, fruit juice, etc.
(c) wine, buffet food, olives, etc.
(d) wine, spirits, peanuts, etc.
(e) cheese cooked with wine, bread, etc.; or small pieces of raw meat to cook yourself at the table
(f) starter or soup, main course, dessert, wine
(g) sandwiches, canapés, soft drinks, wine, etc.
(h) (in the morning) coffee and biscuits; (in the afternoon) coffee or tea and biscuits
(i) a wide selection of wines and cheeses
(j) sandwiches, cakes, strawberries, etc.
(k) turkey, vegetables, potatoes, traditional Christmas pudding, mince pies, wine
(l) charcoal-grilled meat and fish, salads, fruit, beer, etc.

Entertainment 2

---

1. Listening

1.1 Information transfer

Tapescript

Extract 1

(Recorded phone announcement)
Hello, this is Madam Tussaud's Wax Works. The museum is open seven days
a week. From Monday to Friday it opens at 9 and closes at 6. On Saturday it
is open from 9 till 8, and on Sunday from 9 till 5. It takes a minimum of two hours
to go round the museum. Tickets cost £5 for adults and £2.50 for students, children
under 16 and old age pensioners. Admission is free on Mondays. Credit cards
are accepted.

Extract 2

(Radio commercial)
Hi there cowpokes and cowgirls! For a real rootin'-tootin' day in the Wild West
come to Cactus City Wild West Theme Park! Yes, bring the kids along to explore
a real old-time pioneering town. See a shoot-out in the saloon, ride a pony down
Main Street, pan for gold with the prospectors of olden days! We're open April
through September, seven days a week from 10 a.m. to sundown. Only $12 for
adults and $6 for children, or buy a family ticket at $24! What's more, every
Saturday and Sunday we have a real Wild West show. Performances start at 2
p.m. and last for two and a half hours. That's value for money! for only $2 extra
per adult. There are free buses to the park throughout the day every Saturday
and Sunday from Cactus City Centre. Yes sirree, there's a whole heap of fun
waiting for all the family at Cactus City Wild West Theme Park.

Extract 3

(In a tourist office)

A: . . . you see, I'm spending a few days in the city and I'd like to know what's
     on.
B: Yes, well, there's a musical, 'Kiss Me Kate', at the Alhambra Theatre. They
     tell me it's very good.
A: When's it on, exactly?
B: Every night except Sunday. Hold on, let me get the details. . . . Yes, the show
     will run until the beginning of July. It begins at 8 o'clock and lasts two and
     a half hours, finishing at 10.45. There's a matinee on Wednesday and
     Saturday. Performances for the matinee start at 2 and end at 4.45.

A: And how much are the tickets?
B: Tickets are £10, £12.50 and £15.
A: That's a bit expensive.
B: Well you might get a ticket at a reduced price. It says here, 'Some tickets may be available at half price half an hour before the performance starts.'
A: Mm. I'll think about that.

Answers to the listening tasks

Extract 1

Place: Madame Tussaud's Wax Works

Opening days: *seven days a week*

Opening times: Monday to Friday: 9–6
                   Saturday: *9-8*
                   Sunday: *9-5*

Tickets cost: £5 adults *£2.50 students, children under sixteen and old age pensioners*

         Monday — free

Additional information: *two* hours *to go round credit cards accepted*

Extract 2

Place: Cactus City Wild West Theme Park

Opening months: *April through September*

Opening days: *seven days a week*

Opening times: *10 a.m. to Sundown*

Wild West Show takes place: *Saturday and Sunday*

Performances start: *10 a.m.*

Performances last: *2½ hours*

Price of admission: *Adults: $12 Children: $6 Family ticket: $24*

(Wild West Show: *$2* extra per *adult*)

Additional information: *free buses to the park throughout the day every Saturday and Sunday from Cactus City Centre*

146

Extract 3

Place: Alhambra Theatre

Event: *Kiss Me Kate*

Performance days: *Monday –*
Saturday   Matinee days: *Wednesday*
and Saturday

Performance starts: *8 p.m.*   Matinee starts: *2 p.m.*

Performance finishes: *10.45 pm.*   Matinee finishes: *4.45 pm.*

Tickets cost: *£10, £12.50 and £15*

Additional information: *Some tickets may be available at half price* half an hour before the performance starts.

1.2 Dilemma

Tapescript

Extract 4

(In the tourist office)

A: Mm. I'll think about that. The thing is I'm only really free tomorrow night.
B: Is there anything else on then?
A: Yes, of course we have a big football match on tomorrow night — the European Cup. You might still get a ticket.
A: When is the match?
B: It starts at 7.30. Tickets are £12 each. You could phone and reserve a ticket. I believe they take credit cards nowadays.

3. Controlled practice

3.1

A: Ann, I've just got two tickets for the show 'Evita' *on* Tuesday. Would you like to go?

B: Oh, I'd love to. But did you say Tuesday? I've got to work late *on* 29th March.

A: That's OK. Tuesday's the 28th. Anyway, the performance *starts at* 7.30.

B: Lovely. So let's meet *at* 7.15.

A: How about a drink before? There's a bar in the theatre which *opens at* 6.30.

B: OK. Oh, by the way *how long does the performance last?*

A: About three hours. It *ends/finishes at* 10.20. We could have something to eat afterwards. There's a nice Italian restaurant near the theatre which *is open* till midnight.

B: That sounds nice. And *how much are* the tickets?

A: Oh, let's not talk about money now. It's an invitation.

B: Well, we can argue about that later. Anyway, I'll see you *on* Tuesday *at* 6.30, in the bar.

3.2

1. f   2. h   3. c   4. b   5. i   6. d   7. g   8. a   9. j   10. e

3.3

1. I won't *charge* you anything for these books — you can have them for nothing.
2. When I look at the *prices* in the shops they always seem to be getting higher.
3. The *cost* of living is very high in Norway and Sweden.
4. If you are a guest in the Atlantic Hotel there is no extra *charge* for the use of the sports equipment.
5. 'How much did that jacket *cost* you?' 'Only £20 — isn't it cheap?'
6. I got a good *price* for the car I sold.
7. The *cost* of a taxi to the airport is around £12.
8. It *costs* more than £5 to get a good haircut nowadays.
9. If you have goods that people want, you can *charge* a high *price* for them.
10. There was a *charge* of $40 just to get into the nightclub — and that didn't include drinks.

4. Transfer

Student B: You are a businessman or businesswoman visiting Student A's town. You want to find something interesting to do this week. Talk to Student A, who works in the Tourist Office. Ask questions about events this week. Decide which event you want to go to. You only have enough free time to to go to *one* event.

1. Listening

1.1 Information transfer

Tapescript

Call 1

A: Good morning, Park Hotel. May I help you?
B: Hello, could I have Hotel Reservations, please?
A: I'll put you through.
   Park Hotel, Reservations, can I help you?
B: Hello, I'm phoning to ask if you have a room for the 25 August, er, a single room with bath. It would be for ...

Call 2

A: Good morning, Johnson Book Company, may I help you?
B: Good morning, Can I speak to Mr Fox, extension 307, please?
A: Hold the line please. ... Still trying to connect you. ... It's ringing for you now. ... I'm sorry, I'm not getting any reply. Can I take a message?
B: Yes. Perhaps you could tell him that Mr Waddell phoned. That's W-A-D-D-E-L-L. Tell him I'll phone again this afternoon.
A: Thank you Mr Waddell. I'll give Mr Fox the message.

Call 3

A: London Insurance Company, good afternoon.
B: Good afternoon. Can I speak to Miss Brown, Room 225, please?
A: Hold on a moment please. I'll put you through. ... I'm sorry, the number is engaged. Would you like to hold?
B: No, it's all right. I'll phone again later.

	Call 1	Call 2	Call 3
Caller's name:	?	*Mr. Waddell*	?
Company or institution taking the call:	*Park Hotel*	*Johnson Book Co.*	*London Insurance Co.*
Caller wants to speak to:	*Hotel reservations*	*Mr. Fox*	*Miss Brown*
Is the call connected immediately (*yes/no*)	*yes*	*No*	*No*
Is the result: S = 'successful', E = 'engaged', NR = 'no reply'?	*S*	*NR*	*E*
Does the caller leave a message? (*yes/no*)	*No*	*yes*	*No*

1.2 Dilemma

Tapescript

Call 4

A: Mediterranean Transport, can I help you?
B: Hello, can I speak to Mr Marco, please?
A: I'll put you through.
C: Hello, Mr Marco's office.
B: Hello, I'd like to speak to Mr Marco.
C: (hesitant): Er ... well, actually ... Mr Marco is at a meeting at the moment. Is it very urgent ... or shall I ask him to call you back?

3. Controlled practice

3.1

O: Just a moment please. I'll put you through. (3)
O: Good morning. IBF Electronics (1)
C: Hello Louise. This is George Brandt. I wanted to thank you for the report you sent us. (6)
O: Ringing for you now (4)
P: Hello, Louise Blanc speaking (5)
C: Hello, could I speak to Miss Louise Blanc, please? (2)

3.2

Suggested answers

1. Good morning, Esperanza College.
2. Could I speak to the Director of Studies, please?
3. Just a moment, please. I'll put you through.
4. Ringing for you now.
5. Good morning. Maria Primo speaking.
6. Good morning, Ms Primo. I wonder if you can tell me if the results of the English exams have arrived yet?
7. I'm afraid they haven't. But I am expecting them to arrive some time later today.
   OK. In that case I'll call back later.
   Right. Bye.
   Bye.

3.3

1. 'Do you know Joe Brown's number?' 'No, but you can look it up in the *telephone directory.*'
2. Hello, operator. I'd like to make a *long-distance call* to Miss Mary White in Hong Kong. The number is Hong Kong 7227259.
3. 'I don't know Jim's new number — he's just moved house.' 'Well you could get his new number from *Directory Enquiries.*'
4. *Long-distance calls* are usually much more expensive than *local calls.*
5. 'What's the *area code* for Edinburgh?' 'I think it's 031.'
6. 'I haven't got any money to pay for a call to my father.' 'Well, you can make a *transfer-charge call* — that means that he pays for the call.'

4. Transfer

1. **Student B**: You are the switchboard operator at Delifoods. Student A telephones and asks for a certain person. You try to put the call through but the line seems to be out of order. Although you try several times, you cannot get a ringing tone on the line. Offer to take a message, or to phone the caller back.

2. **Student B**: You are the switchboard operator at Beauty Stores. The time now is 14.30. You take the call from Student A (on a very bad line) and after some difficulty put him/her through to the Assistant Manager (Student C). Several urgent calls come in for C while A and C are talking. You interrupt the conversation several times to ask C if he/she wants to take the calls. (You can use sentences like 'I've got Mr Jones on the line from Perfection Lipstick. He says it's very important ...', etc.)

Student C: You are the Assistant Manager at Beauty Stores. The time is 14.30. A call comes through for you, but the line is bad, so you constantly have to ask the caller to repeat the information. From time to time the switchboard operator interrupts your conversation to ask you if you want to take other calls — but you do not think these calls are very important.

You are busy every day of the week this week, except for tomorrow afternoon, or from 9 to 10 in the morning of the day after tomorrow — but that is the time when you go to your weekly golf practice and you do not want to miss it unless there is a good reason.

UNIT 18 **Handling the language**

1. Listening $\boxed{\text{oo}}$

1.1 Information transfer

Tapescript

Dialogue 1

A: A ticket to Cambridge, please
B: Single or return?
A: Sorry? 'Return?'

Dialogue 2

A: Whereabouts do you come from?
B: I ... er ... from my hotel.
A: No, Sorry! I mean whereabouts do you *come* from?
B: Sorry, my English isn't very good. Could you repeat that, please?

Dialogue 3

A: Right! So you take a taxi back. Have a quick wash and change and we'll meet around 8, in the foyer. I'll come and pick you up, OK?
B: Mm.
A: Are you sure you've got that?
B: Sure!

Dialogue 4

A: So, we'll aim to leave before the AGM, if that's alright with you.
B: Sorry? Before the what?
A: The AGM.
B: The AGM did you say? What does AGM stand for?
A: Oh, sorry! Annual General Meeting.
B: Oh, I see. Thanks.

Dialogue 5

A: Get a cab and ask him to take you to 31A Thorndyke Street, Beverley.
B: Er, could you write that down, please?

Answer to the listening task

   Dialogue   Purpose (suggested answers)

1	X	Buying a railway ticket
2	X	Asking which country the person is from
3	✓	Arranging to meet later
4	✓	Arranging to leave
5	X	Giving instructions to get to an address

1.2 Dilemma

Dialogue 6

A: I know a really good joke. It's about the actress and the ...
B: Sorry? Sorry? Actress?
A: Yes, you know, a woman who ...

3. Controlled practice

3.1

One way, or there and back?	1
I'll meet you at your hotel a little later.	3
We'll try to leave early, if you don't mind.	4
Do you really understand?	3
It will be at about 8 o'clock.	3
We needn't stay for the meeting.	4
What country are you from?	2
I'll meet you, and then take you in my car.	3
Take a taxi.	5

3.2

1. A: And of course, you'll need a cross-head screwdriver for this job.
    B: *Sorry?* What kind of screwdriver?
    A: A cross-head screwdriver — one with a cross on the top of it.

2. A: ... and he's the Managing Director of the company.
    B: *Managing Director,* did you say?
    A: Oh yes — he's a Very Important Person.

3. A: Or you could put your money into our Super Saver Account at a guaranteed rate of interest of 2 per cent above the normal rate.
    B: I'm sorry. *Can you write that down, please?*
    A: Oh, sorry. Look, here's a leaflet. It tells you everything. You see? 'Super Saver Account. Two per cent above the normal rate ...'

4. A: So there's this man who goes to market, and he wants to buy a horse, so he goes up to the dealer ...
    B: *'Dealer'?*
    A: That's right — the man who's selling the horses. So he goes to him and ...

154

5. A: So you go along Liberation Street ...
   B: *Mm/Yes.*
   A: And you turn left at the second set of traffic lights ...
   B: *Yes/Mm.*
   A: And you'll see it straight ahead of you.
   B: OK. I've got it.

6. A: Beat the eggs, add a little milk and a pinch of salt and pour the mixture into the pan ...
   B: Sorry, *could you repeat that, please?*
   A: Yes, of course. Beat the eggs, add a little milk and a pinch of salt and pour the mixture into the pan.

3.3

1. I don't understand this sentence. *Could you explain it, please?*
2. *I'm afraid I can't read English very well.* What's this word here?
3. I have to take the underground to Marble Arch. *Can you show it to me please?*
4. Please, not so fast! *Can you speak a little more slowly?*
5. A: Do you believe in precognition?
   B: *I'm sorry, I didn't quite catch the last word.*
   A: Precognition. Do you believe in it?

UNIT 19 **Weather**

1. Listening 〇〇

1.1 Information transfer

Tapescript

Forecast 1

In Southern Europe, especially around the Mediterranean, you are going to have a wet weekend. You may get some very heavy outbreaks of rain in the coastal regions, before brighter, clearer weather arrives at the beginning of next week.

Forecast 2

Over the Alps there will be prolonged snow showers. So, if you are going to spend the weekend skiing, be prepared for some difficult conditions. By Monday the weather is likely to improve with blue skies — ideal conditions for skiing.

Forecast 3

In Central and Northern France the weather will definitely remain grey and cloudy. There may be the occasional shower, but only in exposed places over the hills and high ground. After the weekend rain will move in for a short time from the Mediterranean, but this is unlikely to last beyond Monday evening.

Forecast 4

The best weather this weekend will be over the British Isles. In the South you can expect warm and sunny weather, and temperatures should reach 20 degrees centigrade. In the North it will be sunny, but temperatures aren't expected to rise above 18 degrees centigrade.

Forecast 5

In Northern Germany hold on to your hats this weekend. Wind speeds of up to 70 miles an hour are forecast and gusts might even reach 90 miles an hour.

Forecast 6

The belt of rain which has caused flooding in Southern Scandinavia has now moved away, and the weather this weekend will certainly improve. In general it should be fair and it is likely that some of you will even have a little sunshine.

Forecast 7

Finally over Eastern Europe the weather is expected to be cold and clear over the weekend. Rain is on its way but certainly won't reach the region until the beginning of next week. I wish you all a pleasant weekend.

Answers to the listening task

Sunny	The British Isles
Fair	Southern Scandinavia
Cloudy	Central and Northern France
Rain	Southern Europe
Snow	The Alps
Cold and clear	Eastern Europe
Windy	Northern Germany

1.2 Dilemma

Tapescript

A: Well, what on earth are we going to do with our visitors on Sunday? I was relying on good weather so that we could go to the seaside. I promised to show them a typical resort.

B: And what's the problem?
A: The weather forecast is terrible — it's going to rain all day.
B: Well, we could show them a typical British seaside resort in the rain.

---

3. Controlled practice

3.1

1. In Italy it is likely that rain will fall in the morning.
   In Italy rain is likely to fall in the morning.
2. In Spain temperatures may/might reach 30 degrees.
3. In Sweden snow is unlikely to fall all weekend.
   In Sweden it is unlikely that snow will fall all weekend.
4. In Norway the winds will certainly/definitely die down.
5. In England fog patches are likely to form.
   In England it is likely that fog patches will form.
6. In France drivers may/might face icy roads.
7. In Switzerland the weather is likely to be grey and cold.
   In Switzerland it is likely that the weather will be grey and cold.
8. In Austria the snow certainly won't melt before the afternoon.
9. In Greece thunderstorms will certainly/definitely develop in the evening.
10. In Germany the snow is unlikely to stop.
    In Germany it is unlikely that the snow will stop.

3.3

Suggested answers

1. A: It's tipping it down out there!
   B: Yes, I *got soaked* this morning!

2. A: Rather dull today!
   B: Yes, *miserable weather*!

3. A: Lovely day today!
   B: Hmmm. *Better than yesterday, don't you think?*

4. A: Chilly, isn't it?
   B: Chilly? It's absolutely *freezing*!

5. A: Hot, isn't it?
   B: Yes, *it's scorching*!

4. Transfer

Student B: You work in a travel office in London. You have had a lot of enquiries about travel because the weather has been very bad recently with storms and floods. Many services are not running and many roads are closed. Student A is going to ring you to ask about travel up to Leeds. Below is the information that you should use to answer the questions. The information in brackets indicates the degree of likelihood.

Flights to Leeds	Departure time
BM102	08.00 (certainly not)
BM103	12.00 (probably not)
BM104	14.00 (possibly)

Rail to Leeds Departures	Bus to Leeds Departures	Roads — passable
08.00 (certainly not)	09.00 (possibly)	motorways a.m. (possibly)
09.00 (probably not)	12.00 (probably)	motorways p.m. (probably)
10.00 (possibly)	14.00 (certainly)	other roads (certainly not)
11.00 (possibly)		
12.00 (probably)		

UNIT 20 Public announcements

1. Listening 🎧

1.1 Information transfer

Tapescript

Announcement 1

British Airways regrets to announce that the 10.30 flight BA701 to New York has been delayed, due to technical problems. The plane will now leave at 12.00 hours. Passengers are invited to proceed to the restaurant, where light refreshments are being served on production of boarding cards.

Announcement 2

Good evening, ladies and gentlemen. This is your captain speaking. We are now cruising at an altitude of 36,000 feet. On take-off I was informed that the radar equipment developed technical problems earlier this morning. Therefore we will experience a short delay in landing, but we should be on the ground by 19.30 local time. Your chief steward will now tell you about landing-card formalities.

Good evening. This is your chief steward. All passengers are required to complete their landing cards now and these will be collected in a few minutes. You may need to refer to your passports to complete the cards. Please write your name, passport number and issue details now. . . . This flight is BA989 and you are all on a block visa. The number is 0437L. The visa is valid for fourteen days. I am sure you will all have a pleasant fortnight, and I hope you will enjoy the rest of the flight.

Announcement 3

This is an announcement for passengers travelling to York. Some of this evening's trains have been cancelled or delayed. We regret any inconvenience caused. The 19.00 train to York from platform 4 has been cancelled. The 20.00 will now leave at 21.00. Further information can be obtained from rail staff at platform 6, where the train is expected to arrive in 30 minutes' time. So the 19.00 to York won't run, and the 20.00 will leave from platform 6 at 21.00.

Announcement 4

This is your chief steward speaking. We are pleased to announce that the buffet car will be open after leaving Peterborough at 22.00. However, due to staff shortages, it will close after leaving Doncaster at 23.30. Because of industrial action some items of food and drink were not delivered to this train. As a result tea, coffee and cold sandwiches will be served, but no beer, lager or other alcoholic drinks are available.

Answers to the listening task

Announcement 1

Departures

Destination	Flight	Departure	Gate	Notes
Delhi	BA135	10.00	27	Delayed till 11.00
Karachi	BA147	10.10	32	Now boarding
New York	BA001	10.30		Delayed till 12.00
Nassau	BA233	11.00	11	Go to gate
Pittsburg	BA217	11.45		

Announcement 2

LANDING CARD

Please complete clearly in BLOCK CAPITALS

Family name: *CHICHUGU*

Forename: *POL*

Passport number: *029988 LR*

Issued on: *11 MARCH 1988*

Issued at: *ROTONGA*

Valid till: *11 MARCH 1998*

Flight number: *BA 989*

Visa number: *0437 L*

Validity: *14 DAYS*

Signature: *Pol Chichugu*

```
                    Train Departures

Destination Departure time Platform Notes
York              19.00            4     Cancelled
York              20.00            6     Departure time: 21.00
```

```
Buffet open from 22.00 to 23.30
Food and drink available:
Tea        ✓
Coffee        ✓
Beer       X
Lager      X
Other alcoholic drinks       X
Cold sandwiches       ✓
```

1.2 Dilemma

Tapescript

Announcement 5

We regret to announce that due to an air traffic control strike all afternoon flights have been cancelled. Flights may resume at 19.00 hours, but we are unlikely to know the situation until 18.00 hours. Passengers travelling to Barona may take a bus from outside the airport building. The bus will arrive at Barona at 22.00.

3. Controlled practice

3.1

1. We are preparing for take-off. (c)
2. We have just landed at London Heathrow airport. (e)
3. We regret to announce a delay of about one hour. (a)
4. Final call for flight BA079. (d)
5. In a few minutes we will be handing out landing cards. (b)

3.2

1. More details can be obtained from the information desk.
2. This claim form must be filled in now.
3. The flight schedule had to be changed for technical reasons.
4. The fault in the equipment has now been corrected.
5. The plane is expected to leave at 19.30.
6. Your luggage was delivered to the hotel this morning.
7. All heavy articles should be placed in the overhead lockers.
8. Only one item of hand luggage can be taken on board.

3.3

1. We are pleased to inform you that ... G
2. The buffet car is situated at the rear of the train. N
3. We regret to announce that ... B
4. We are happy to be able to tell you that ... G
5. Will all passengers holding blue boarding cards please proceed to the aircraft now. N
6. The bar will be open from 2 p.m. till 6 p.m. N
7. We are sorry that this will cause some inconvenience. B
8. Unfortunately this is beyond our control. B

4. Transfer

Suggested answers

W = written; S = spoken

1. Tickets, please. (S) bus or train
2. End of season bargains. (W) shop or store
3. Last orders, please. (S) pub
4. Vacant. (W) toilet
5. Guests are requested to vacate their rooms by midday. (W) hotel
6. Please extinguish all cigarettes. (S) plane
7. Mind the doors. (S) tube/underground railway, train or bus
8. Please do not disturb. (W) hotel
9. Baggage should not be left unattended at any time. (S) airport
10. Books may be renewed by post or phone. (W) library